# *The*
# UNDERGROUND
# RAILROAD
## *on*
# LONG ISLAND

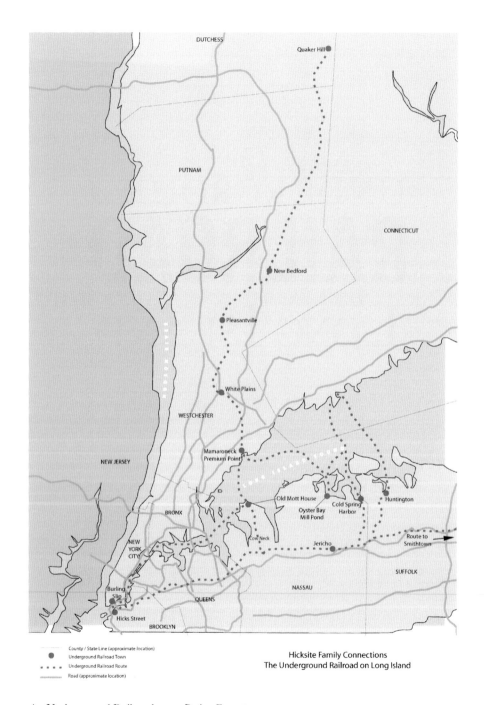

Hicksite Family Connections
The Underground Railroad on Long Island

An Underground Railroad map. *Desiree Fumento.*

*The*
# UNDERGROUND
# RAILROAD
## *on*
# LONG ISLAND
## FRIENDS IN FREEDOM

KATHLEEN G. VELSOR

THE
History
PRESS

Published by The History Press
Charleston, SC 29403
www.historypress.net

Copyright © 2013 by Kathleen G. Velsor
All rights reserved

First published 2013

Manufactured in the United States

ISBN 978.1.60949.770.5

Library of Congress CIP data applied for.

*To my mother and father,*
*Doris Beal Gaffney and Matthew Watson Gaffney Sr.*

# CONTENTS

# ACKNOWLEDGEMENTS

I am extremely appreciative of the many people who have opened their hearts and minds to me during the course of my research on the Underground Railroad on Long Island. I have had the opportunity to meet and work with many kind and generous people who have given their time to share stories and opened their homes and private collections to me in anticipation that I would share their family stories.

I am extremely grateful to Jim Driscoll and Richard Hourahan from the Queens Historical Society and to Dr. Wini Warren and Terry Walton from Rosalie Inc. Productions for their encouragement in the early phases of my research. I am thankful to my sister, Dr. Margaret G. Benedict, director of the Matthew W. Gaffney Foundation, for her spirit and encouragement to write this book. The many hours of conversation spent with Leon Rushmore from the Westbury Friends Meeting will always be precious to me. He was truly a Friend, sharing valuable information so that I could pass it on to others. I was truly honored to have known Jean Renison, curator, who was always giving me ideas to help direct my research using the documents at the Westbury Historical Library. I very much appreciate the assistance of Dr. Christopher Densmore from Swarthmore College Library; thank you for always answering my questions. Thanks to Dr. Lynda Day, professor at Brooklyn College, for sharing the letter from Wilmer about the Underground Railroad on Long Island. Thanks to Doris Pallet for knowing about the secret door at the Maine Maid Inn. Sincere appreciation goes to Robert MacKay and Charla Bolton, from the Society for the Preservation of Long

Island Antiquities, for taking the initiative to work with the Village of Old Westbury and save the "Old Place."

Many thanks to Kathryn and Thomas Abbey, members of the Jericho Friends Meeting, for their encouragement and support; Betsey Murphy, Jericho Library, for her continual help and knowledge about Jericho; Michael Butkewicz, Nassau County Parks, for his guidance and assistance to view the grounds of the Jericho Preserve; Marty Schackner, Nassau County Parks, who graciously opened the doors to the Elias Hicks House and the Jackson/Malcolm Home; and Ellen and Rich Benson, who opened their home on Mill Hill, told many stories and provided me with the opportunity for photographs.

Thanks to Jennifer McHugh from the Wantagh Library; members of the Nassau County Archives; the Oyster Bay Historical Society; the Rheese Library, University of Rochester; the Frederick County Historical Society; and the Guilford College Library Friends Collection in Greensboro, North Carolina.

Special appreciation goes to the State University of New York–Old Westbury and the College Foundation for granting numerous research grants to travel and document the stories of the Underground Railroad on Long Island. Thanks also go to the members of the Underground Railroad Teaching Partnership for their encouragement—Desiree Fumento for the map of the Underground Railroad; Gerri Faivre, head of Westbury Friends School; and Suzy Shechtman of Schechtman Productions. Special thanks go to Michael Kinane, assistant to the president for advancement, for his continuous support of this research and to Dr. Calvin O. Butts III, president of the College of Old Westbury and senior pastor at Abyssinian Baptist Church, for his continual interest and support of this project.

Most of all, thanks to my husband, Curtis F. Velsor Jr., whose Quaker family roots helped to open doors to the hidden records and secret stories of the work of the early Long Island Quakers. I greatly appreciate Curt's encouragement. He has traveled every road, talked to numerous historians, looked for documents, searched for hidden records and papers, climbed ladders, taken photographs and listened to every story many times. Thank you.

# INTRODUCTION

The story of the Underground Railroad on Long Island is the story about two groups of people. One story is about the formation of the Society of Friends, first in England and later on Long Island. The other story involves the capture and sale of the Africans and their transport to the early settlers in New York. Both stories are about oppression and the search for independence that brought them to Long Island.

As a young child, I lived in a small town in upstate New York. I remember hearing stories about the Underground Railroad and finding them fascinating. Forty years later, while researching this topic at the Long Island Studies Institute, I was handed a copy of a Xerox letter addressed to Wilmer and dated August 4, 1939, seen here and also transcribed:

*Laurel Hill Road*
*Northport, N.Y., 8/4/39*

Dear Wilmer:

*I'm returning that very remarkable book. "Quaker Hill." Lay it aside to read when thee has time. So many names I know. There is my Aunt Phebe J Wanzer, there father of David Irish. His home was the last Station on the Underground R.R. My mothers' home, Joseph Carpenter of New Rochelle, was the first Station out of New York City. My fathers, Joseph Pierce, Pleasantville, was the second Station. Judge John Jay, Bedford, was the third station, this aunt's home. David Irish,*

Letter to Wilmer from Jonathan, August 4, 1939. *Haviland Records Room, Swarthmore College Library.*

*Quaker Hill was the fourth Station. At that place—60 miles from N.Y. the fugitives were far enough on the way to Canada, to find their way safely. These Quakers were the force that finally got the Yearly Meeting to decide that no Friend could hold slaves. And yet the writer of the book is so far from understanding of the great mind that he is dealing with that he tells us those people live in a mental attitude of make believe.*[1]

Many questions came quickly to mind. Where is Quaker Hill? Who was David Irish? Is Jonathan's last name Pierce? What I discovered was that I was as equally enthralled with this period of history in 1994 as I was as a child. Since then, I have written numerous grants to prove that Long Island Quakers were involved in the Underground Railroad. Throughout my travels, I have met many historians and collected numerous letters and original notes from universities, historical collections and private sources. I have found that these stories were recorded by early abolitionists and freedom seekers and were even hidden in numerous locations. My quest has been challenging, and it helped me to conclude that many families helped to establish a freedom trail running throughout Long Island. The struggle for freedom was not guaranteed, but it was fought by many. This work intends to retell the stories of the many people who worked to help others to circumvent oppression.

# THE BEGINNING

This is a story that reflects Long Island's resources, political foundation, location and topography. The politics began as early as 1641, when the first settlers arrived on Long Island. These settlers were English and were sent from Connecticut to start another Presbyterian community. The founders of what is now called Hempstead were Robert Coe, Richard Gilderssleeve, Edmund Jeremial, Jonas Wood, Thomas Weeks and John Seaman.

When the early settlers arrived on Long Island, they found open fields, or plains. These geographic features were formed by two glaciers. Gravel and sand deposits left rich topsoil at a shallow depth, so mature trees could not grow. Tall grasses grew on the plains instead, providing a natural open space for farming and grazing cattle. As was the custom in England, large areas were set aside for common pastures. Each animal was marked to identify ownership, and various people were assigned the tasks of fencing and watching the livestock. Plots were allotted for farming needed vegetables. Bernice Schultz, author of *Colonial Hempstead*, described the south plains where the land gently sloped to the Atlantic Ocean:

> *As the plains meet the sea level the ground water comes to the service converting the edge of the plain into a vast marsh which stretches fifty miles from Coney Island to Islip. The landward edge of the marsh is usually a continuous meadow which shades off with an intermingling of fresh and brackish water vegetation into a salt marsh where the salt water seepage dominates across the southern edge of the town, and is broken up by a multitude of irregular inlets and creeks, was valued for its salt hay which served as relish for cattle and was cut in the late summer by farmers who transported great loads of it by boat.*[2]

Next to the "edge of the plains" along the north shore of Long Island were woodlands with large trees for shelter and kettle ponds for water. Many of the early settlers built their homes around these sources of fresh water.

Some of the ponds can still be seen today. There is a pond in the center of Post Road just north of Jericho Turnpike that was the site of one of the early Quaker settlements and that remains a tribute to an earlier lifestyle. (Rather, Post Road separates around a large pond.)

The north shore of Long Island had many small creeks that ran through marshlands. During the early summer and fall, these are decorated with tall sea grasses that identify the width of the tidal areas. Many of these wetlands were preserved during the 1970s, but until that time, some buildings, roads and beaches were established that blur the perspective that the early settlers may have seen. Many tidal marshes were sites of Long Island mills. Products such as corn and flour needed to be processed, as well as lumber from trees. The movement of the tidal waters helped to provide the source of power. During the 1700s, there were more than three hundred mills on the north shore of Long Island. Some of these mills were operated by early Quakers.

# THE SOCIETY OF FRIENDS ON LONG ISLAND

*He walked the dark world in the mild*
*Still guidance of the Light:*
*In tearful tenderness a child,*
*A strong man in the right.*
*—Thomas C. Cornell*[3]

Thomas Cornell was a Quaker from birth. After questioning his faith, Cornell realized that his life's work was to record the history of his early relatives. His book *Adam and Anne Mott: Their Ancestors and Their Descendants* proved to be invaluable to finding the basis for this story. To understand the history, it's helpful to know more about who the Quakers were.

In 1647, a man known as George Fox began to challenge some of the ideas set in the Calvinist claim that all people were caught up in sin. He was confused by the doctrines and felt that he needed to separate himself from the strict conduct set by the Anglican Church—and thus separate his family and community, too. At the time, he was a young man in his twenties, and he wanted to come to his own understanding of his relationship with God. As a result, he spent a year in meditation looking for answers. He emerged from seclusion espousing his belief that the word of God did not need to be interpreted by a pastor, priest, minister or rabbi, but rather each man could hear the divine spirit by sitting quietly and listening. He preached to large groups of people in open fields under public scrutiny. He spoke about his year of meditation, saying that he had a series of experiences, which he referred to as "openings," that he interpreted as the divine spirit speaking directly to him. He felt compelled to share these experiences.

He traveled around Europe in 1647, debating the established theology in an effort to convert others. George Fox was jailed for blasphemy in Derby, England, yet he continued to actively seek followers as soon as he was released from prison. In 1652, the Society of Friends (often known as Quakers) was formally established, and a change in attitude among other Christians began to take place. The basic belief that God can speak directly to any man or women meant that the divine spirit could speak to all people.

This belief that individuals can participate in a direct dialogue with God—first promulgated among English Quakers by Fox—is understood to mean that each person is responsible for his/her own actions. Fox and his followers were persecuted for espousing these beliefs; as a result, many Quakers left Europe in search of religious freedom.[4]

The Quakers believed that the New World would offer them a greater opportunity for religious freedom; some traveled to New Amsterdam (New York today) and then to a Dutch colony administered by the Dutch West India Company. At that time, the Netherlands—the most prosperous of the European countries—was having difficulty luring a sufficient number of people to its American colony to make it economically viable. Dutch leaders believed that it was in their own financial interest to accept settlers from a variety of sources, even those considered to be religious dissenters in other places. Because no one else would go, they accepted a group composed of Quakers that arrived in New Amsterdam on Robert Fowler's ship *Woodhouse* on August 6, 1657.[5]

The Quakers came to the New World because they believed that they would have the freedom to express their principles. The English ship *Woodhouse* landed at the colony on a Saturday, and the next day, two members of the group paid a visit to New Amsterdam governor Peter Stuyvesant to explain their mission. Stuyvesant appeared "moderate both in words and actions," but clearly their assessment of him was misguided. As early as 1653, Stuyvesant had been pronouncing a series of stricter and stricter edicts. Flushing leaders had joined with leaders in other places (three English towns and four Dutch towns) to send petitions of remonstrance to Stuyvesant denouncing his rules and asserting their right to participate in lawmaking. Heartened by their group leaders' initial positive assessment of Stuyvesant, two Quaker preachers—Mary Weatherhead and Dorthy Waugh—left the *Woodhouse* and took to the streets. They began preaching their beliefs as they walked up and down the streets of New Amsterdam. With loud voices, they drew a crowd of local residents in response to their words. Stuyvesant then declared the women's behavior to be disruptive, and Mary and Dorthy were arrested and put in prison. They stayed for eight days and then were physically removed from the city of New Amsterdam. The women were handcuffed, taken back to the *Woodhouse* and deported to Rhode Island.[6]

Robert Hodgson, a Quaker who had also arrived on the *Woodhouse*, went on to the English colony at Gravesend. His testimonies were well received there by local settlers, who had originally come from Massachusetts and who were said to harbor "Quaker proclivities." Hodgson later traveled east on Long Island, first to Jamaica and then to Hempstead, visiting people's homes, where he "rejoiced in the telling of those living truths which were preached among them." While in Hempstead, Hodgson began organizing his first gathering of Friends, which he planned to hold in a local orchard. Since Governor Stuyvesant had seriously rethought his position on the usefulness of Quaker dissenters, he notified Justice of the Peace Richard Gildersleeve to stop any Quaker meetings and arrest Hodgson. Hodgson was subsequently captured at the start of the first day's Sunday meeting in the orchard and detained in a private home.[7] Despite his arrest, the religious service continued. Henry Onderdonk recounted, "The strong willed Quaker outwitted the magistrate; for during his absence the prisoner, by his loud voice and energetic action, (Probably in preaching out the window) had collected a large crowd of listeners who stayed and heard the truth declared."[8]

The next day, Hodgson and two women—one with a "baby at her Breast"—were taken under military escort from Hempstead to the governor in New Amsterdam, about twenty miles away. During the trip, the women were allowed to sit in the cart, but Hodgson was handcuffed to the cart and dragged along an open field and the dirt trails that were used as roads. Onderdonk recounted, "As [a] part of his journey was performed in darken night, need we wonder that it was a painful to the prisoners, and Hodgson's arms were chafed by the briars and brambles that invested the path."[9]

Local residents of Flushing soon became afraid of similar gatherings and felt that the Quakers were too outspoken. Consequently, Governor Stuyvesant, fearing that the Quakers would not adhere to the Dutch form of Protestantism, passed an anti-Quaker law forbidding any resident from entertaining a Quaker in New Amsterdam. The fine was set at fifty pounds. Henry Townsend, a Quaker resident of Flushing, was fined for allowing his home to be used as a meeting place. Outraged, he gained the support of

Edward Hart, the town clerk, who wrote a document condemning the law. Known as the *Flushing Remonstrance*, it begins with this paragraph:

> *You have been pleased to send unto us a certain prohibition or command that we should not receive or entertain any of those people called Quakers because they are supposed to be, by some, seducers of the people. For our part we cannot condemn them in this case, neither can we stretch out our hand against them, for out of Christ God is a consuming fire, and it is a fearful thing to fall into the hands of the living God. Therefore if any of these said persons (Quakers) come in love unto us, we cannot in conscience lay violent hands upon them, but give them, free egress and regresse unto our town and houses, as God shall persuade consciences and in this we are true subjects both of church and State, for we are bounde be the law of God and man to doe good unto all men and evil to no man. And this is according to the patent and charter of our towne, given unto us in the name of the States General, which we are not will to infringe and violate, but shall houlde to our patent and shall remaine, your humble subjects, the inhabitants of Vlishing [sic].*[10]

On December 27, 1657, thirty-one citizens signed the petition, giving proof to the belief that people should have the right to choose their own religion. This action did not go without punishment for Flushing town officers and leaders. Official maltreatment of Quakers (and the Quakers' own passive reaction to that treatment) set the stage for the conversion of many residents of Flushing to the Society of Friends. One such conversion was that of John Bowne, who was converted to Quakerism by his wife, Hannah Feake, from Oyster Bay.

In the earliest days, Friends like John Bowne and Hannah Feake attended secret Society of Friends meetings in the woods. Originally named the Oyster Bay Meeting, the Flushing Meeting was represented at and subject to the General Meeting of Rhode Island. In his diary, John Bowne wrote, "On the 11th and 4th month, 1661, we went from our house toward Rhode Island, to the General Meeting, where we stayed nine days and on the 28th we came home again." According to the minutes of the Rhode Island General Meeting, Bowne was arrested on August 24, 1662, for holding Sunday meetings. He was taken to New Amsterdam, where he was kept in prison for refusing to pay his fine, although he later escaped when his prison cell door was left unlocked. He refused to obey the dictates set by Governor Peter Stuyvesant and was formally sent back to England and then to Holland, where he stood trial and was found not guilty. Furthermore, the verdict soon set by the Dutch West India Company instructed Stuyvesant to adopt a more lenient position toward religious freedom: "The conscience of men at least ought even to remain free and unshackled." In 1667, when the English took over the colony and renamed it New York, John Bowne was allowed to return to his home in Flushing. This experience made John Bowne "forever after a leading Friend."[11]

With such unrest in Flushing, Quakers began to move east to Long Island to settle in the rich farmlands of the North Shore and avoid persecution for their beliefs and their refusal to pay taxes to support the Anglican Church of England. Henry Townsend was the first to leave Flushing and come to Oyster Bay, and many followed. As these communities grew, so did the Society of Friends. By 1672, George Fox had made another trip to New York to visit new members. Norman Pennpacker's journal recorded the event. George Fox came by flatboat from New York to Gravesend. He traveled with a group of men, and they brought their horses, as was the custom. "[We] got that evening to Friends at Gravesend with whom we Tarried that night and the next day got to Flushing, to one John Bowne's who was banished by the Dutch." Fox then traveled to Oyster Bay, where he attended a six-day-long General Meeting of the Friends.

Next to the millpond on Lake Avenue in Oyster Bay, there is a historic marker at Council Rock. The sign relates that the site is where George Fox first addressed the Friends. Noted on the sign are the names Feeks, Townsend and Weeks. These families still live in Oyster Bay. Returning to Flushing, Fox visited again with John Bowne before traveling to New England. He recorded in his journal how pleased he was to see so many Quakers: "And many hundreds of the world were there and were much satisfied and desired to hear again and said that if I came to their town I should have their meeting place, they were so loving. And a justice of the peace was there and his family and many considerable persons were there. A glorious heavenly meeting it was, praised be the God, and the people were much satisfied."[12] George Fox continued to travel extensively throughout the colonies in 1672–73. As a result, the membership in the Society of Friends increased considerably.[13]

As George Fox traveled through colonial America, he began to question the institution of slavery. He spoke out often, saying that the slaves were stolen property in the same category as "prize goods" forcibly taken by pirates. He warned that dealing in such illegal materials or any products produced by slave labor violated Quaker ethics. He suggested that "after certain years of servitude, they [the Friends] should make them [slaves] free."[14] Irish Quaker William Edmundson also came to the New York Yearly Meeting at this time, and he pointed out the inconsistency of opposing the enslavement of Indian prisoners captured in King Philip's War while still owning persons of African origin. He encouraged Friends to think about what it would be like to be enslaved.[15]

In 1688, the German Mennonites who had settled in Pennsylvania also voiced concern regarding slavery. They asked, "What thing can be done worse toward us than if men should steal us away and sell us for slaves to strange country separating husbands from their wives and children? Who profess that it is not lawful to steal…must avoid to purchase [men stolen by robbers]…and such men should be delivered out of Ye hand of ye robbers and set free."[16] This group challenged the Quakers, saying, "Then is Pennsylvania to have a good report; instead it has now a bad one for this sake in other countries. Especially whereas the Europeans are desirous to know in what manner the Quakers do rule in their province, and most of them do look upon us with an envious eye. But if this is done well, what shall we say is done evil?"[17]

One wonders how the Quakers who had settled in Oyster Bay responded to this statement. To help answer this question, my research took me to the Westbury Historical Society. This is a wonderful collection of volumes, letters, diaries and various donated and acquired documents. The historical collection is located in the small brick building known as "the Cottage," nestled between the children's library and the main library. When I arrived at the library, it was a beautiful summer day. The door was closed, but I gave it a little knock. Just as I was about to leave, I heard the lock turn, and the screen door slowly opened. Peeking between the door and the screen was a slim-faced woman with dark eyes and a gentle smile. I soon knew her to be Miss Jeannie Renison. I started with my questions, and as quickly as I asked them, Jeannie had disappeared into the back room. I could hear the shuffle of papers, and suddenly she reappeared with the answers. In response to my questions about slavery on Long Island, she uncovered a file box labeled "The Hicks Family Papers." One item was a speech. In 1941, Henry Hicks of Hicks Nursery made a speech at the 77th anniversary of the freeing of the slaves and the 100th anniversary of the Westbury Firehouse. Henry Hicks made the record clear that Long Island Quakers were struggling with the moral questions concerning slavery.

Just as voices were speaking out in the Westbury Meeting, others were being heard by Quakers in Oyster Bay, who began to take action. In 1685, one of the first manumissions was recorded. "In 1685 'Tom, ye Negro' was freed. And in 1700 'Dick' was freed and there are many evidences of deep conscience prickings during the 1700s. At Yearly Meeting as early as 1716, several Friends declared that they were fully satisfied in their consciences that yet set practice was not Rite [*sic*]."[18] Since Long Island Quakers did not need to own large number of slaves to work on their farms and homes, the moral dilemma of freeing slaves was not as great an economic necessity for them as it was in the South.[19]

By 1720, the slave population ratio on Long Island was about one slave for every ten settlers. Some Quakers argued that as long as they fed and provided shelter, education and employment for their slaves, slavery was acceptable. A change in attitude started in 1749 when John Wolman, a Quaker minister, traveled through New York.[20] He had just finished writing "Considerations of the Keeping of Negroes," in which he argued that slavery was against the beliefs of the Society of Friends. Westbury's Amos Powell was so moved by Wolman's ideas that he traveled with him on his ministry throughout the New England area. As a result, the following year, the New York Meeting decided that no Quaker could import slaves.[21]

As I continued to read about the chain of events that was taking place at the Yearly Meeting in Flushing, I noticed that the first query concerning slavery came from Quaker Hill. I remembered from a Johnathan Pierce letter, dated 1939, that Quaker Hill was one of the last stops going north on the Underground Railroad. So where was Quaker Hill, also known as the Oblong, and why was this important?

In about 1740, New York Quakers began to settle in Westchester County. Many of these families were from Long Island, and some Quakers came from Massachusetts, where the politics of the predominant church of Congregationalists were infringing on the religious beliefs of the members of the Society of Friends. Purchase Monthly Meeting was the first to be recognized by the New York Meeting in the Hudson River Valley. Then New Milford, Connecticut Monthly Meeting asked Purchase Monthly Meeting to be recognized. The settlement at the Oblong began as the result of boundary disputes between the Dutch settlements in the Hudson River Valley and the English settlements in Connecticut. The "Oblong Patent," as it was called, was a deliberate attempt to separate the English and the Dutch settlers, who were continually at odds with one another. The Oblong was a strip of land one and three-quarters miles wide extending from East Greenwich, Connecticut, north to what is now the Massachusetts state line. The settlement was an ideal location for Quakers looking to separate themselves from other religious groups. The meeting that was formed is

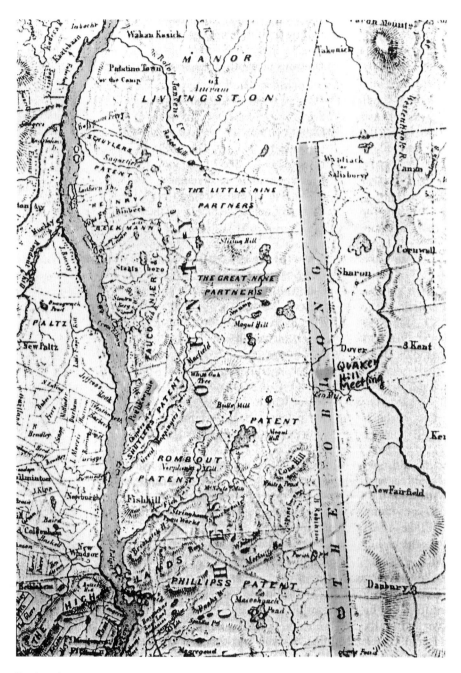

Portion of a 1779 map depicting counties, manors, patents and townships in the Oblong.

referred to as the Oblong, and the settlement became known as Quaker Hill. Quaker Hill is near present-day Pawling, New York, off Route 22 half a mile up a hill overlooking the Hudson River Valley. The original meetinghouse is still standing and is registered as a National Landmark, a citation that acknowledges these Quakers for speaking out against slavery. The members of the Quaker Hill Meeting did not own slaves and had strong feelings about holding people in bondage.[22]

David Irish Sr. presented the first public slavery statement after the close of the Quarterly Meeting. As with the vast majority of Quaker statements, this statement on slavery was presented in the form of a formal "query" on May 30, 1767, at the New York Yearly Meeting held at the Flushing Meetinghouse. The query stated simply, "Relation to buying and Selling Negroes: It is not Consistent with Christianity to buy and sell our Fellowman for Slaves during their Lives & Posterities after them, then whether it is consistent with a Christian Spirit to keep in slavery that we have already in possession by Purchase, Gift or any otherways."[23]

The following year, an essay—formulated by a committee and approved by the membership of the New York Yearly Meeting—presented a public pronouncement in response to the Oblong query:

Quaker Hill Meeting. *Velsor Collection.*

Inside the Quaker Hill Meeting. *Velsor Collection.*

*We are of the mind that it is not convenient (considering the circumstances of things amongst us) to give an answer to this Query, at least at this time, as the answering of it in direct terms manifestly tends to cause Strife amongst us, which ought to be Avoided, and Charity exercise, and persuasive methods pursued and that which make for peace. We are however full of the mind that Negroes as Rational Creatures are by born free, and where the way opens liberty ought to be extended to them, and they not held in Bondage self ends. But to turn them out at large, indiscriminately, which seems to be the tendency of the Query, will we apprehend, Be attended with great inconveniency, as some are too young and some too old to obtain a livelihood for themselves.*[24]

The 1768 response from the New York Yearly Meeting, while supporting the same ideals presented in the Oblong query, was significantly watered down, focusing on the "inconveniency" of freeing slaves who might not be able to earn their own livelihood.[25] The practical issue of the time was that if a man neglected to support a former enslaved person, that former slave could be sent to paupers' prison or jail.

While Quakers were trying to deal with the moral and economic issues surrounding slavery, the slave population ratio on Long Island in 1773 had grown to one slave for every five settlers. The members of the Flushing Meeting took a firmer stand, urging members not to purchase slaves. Elias Hicks, a Quaker from Jericho, Long Island, attended that meeting representing the Westbury Friends Meeting. He stood during the meeting and spoke with a firm voice, reminding members that the Quaker community should disown anyone who continued to buy or sell slaves or who permitted those who came of age to remain slaves.[26]

Benjamin Lay included the following sentiment in his 1773 *All Slave-keepers* publication to Friends: "Friends were to do unto others as they would want to have done to them." Richard Burlings's paper that spoke against slavery was included in this publication. Although there was conflict on the two sides of the issue of abolition among Friends, each side was able to find some rationalization for its position—some said that they fed, sheltered and employed their slaves, thus protecting them from harsher treatment, while others believed that no reasonable person would want to be enslaved.[27]

Between 1775 and 1776, 85 slaves were freed by the members of the Westbury Meeting. In 1776, the Westbury Friends Meeting appointed Elias Hicks and Gideon Seaman to meet with those Quaker families who still had slaves to discuss their manumission. Through their efforts, 154 manumissions had been recorded by 1791 in Queens County.[28] Among the manumissions were those recorded by members Samuel Willis, Phebe Willets Mott Dodge, John Hicks (the father of Elias Hicks) and Ester (Williams) Seaman.[29]

The Hicks Family Papers collection recorded members' reasons for manumitting slaves, some of which are of particular interest because they exemplify the growing antislavery sentiments that had taken root among the Westbury Friends. These reasons also express recognition of the need to educate former enslaved people in a trade to ensure that they would be able to fend for themselves after being manumitted: "[I] Phebe Dodge being possessed of a Negro Woman named Rachael am fully Satisfied it be my duty as also a Christian act to set her at liberty…Samuel Hicks frees James when he arrives at the age of 24 years, he having agreed to live with John Carle to serve him after the manner of an apprentice to Learn his Trade of a Joiner."

Other Friends purchased slaves solely for the purpose of setting them free: "[I] William Loines sets my Negro man Lige Free whom I purchased for the purpose of freeing him. Peaceably enjoying all his Estate he may acquire from me." Loines also freed a man named Israel and said that a man named Isaac "had his liberty at the Age of 21." Thomas Seaman, son of Nathaniel Seaman, "[bought] one Negro man named Jacob, about 40 years old, for

£40 in order to set him free." William Mott wrote that he had already freed his slave Amey but stated that he knew that for her own safety in the future, there would need to be a record of her manumission: "[I] William Mot frees ten slaves, among them Amey, several years ago [I] did give unto my Negro woman named Amey her freedom and [she] has [had] her freedom ever since. Therefore I do confirm unto her."

The list contains some first names among those being freed—Mingo, Ponder, Cato, Plato, Likeum, Lige, Grandus, Tobey, Obod, Mareah, Sambo, Izzabel, Sibyll, Chloe, Neptune, York, Hagar, Primus and Easter— as well as more biblical names such as Elijah, Israel and Amey. None of the manumitted slaves had a last name, but upon being freed, many took the names or parts of names from their former owners. This explains why today there are many African Americans who still live in the Westbury-Jericho area who bear the surnames Hicks, Jackson, Rushmore, Underhill and Willis. In many cases, they are the descendants of those who continued to work for Friends. In a number of instances, though, slave-owning Quakers, while acknowledging that slavery was ultimately antithetical to Friends' beliefs, were reluctant to manumit their own slaves. These Quakers followed the gradual approach, which they deemed similar to George Fox's.[30]

The struggle for personal freedom intensified for the Quakers during the Revolutionary War. At the outbreak of the war in 1775, the Revolutionary army was composed mainly of volunteers. When the colonies declared their independence, each enacted its own military draft laws. The New York legislature recognized Quaker antiwar beliefs and granted Quaker men an exemption from military service—without payment of fines—as long as they could present a certification of membership from the monthly Friends Meeting. After the Declaration of Independence was signed in 1777, New York revised its laws so that the section on military service now allowed exemptions for Quakers only on the condition that money be paid as a substitute for military service. All Quaker males could be considered for military exemption, but each would have to pay ten pounds annually if called to service. If Quakers did not pay, their livestock could be taken or they could be jailed until payment was made. By 1778, the fines had increased fivefold; by 1780, they had increased eightfold. Despite the heavy tax, Quaker pacifist testimonies continued.[31]

As the war progressed, many Long Island residents came to resent the Quakers. Pro- and anti-Quaker sentiments divided communities. To make matters worse, Quakers themselves quickly became divided, with some remaining pacifist and some feeling that they should help defend their communities against the British. Quaker homes were subject to British occupation. Meetinghouses were occupied by British troops, and some were destroyed. In 1778, British soldiers seized the Flushing Meetinghouse and used it as a prison, hospital and storage space for hay.[32]

That same year, the British requested wood for heat and hay for their horses from the Westbury Friends, which they refused to give. Both the Flushing and Westbury Friends Meetings stated that they could "neither obey such orders nor receive payment for such articles requisitioned." With the increase in the war effort, many Quakers remained loyal to their testimonies, yet many did not. Quaker families became separated due to participation in the war effort, with some members enlisting on one side or the other while others maintained a pacifist testimony. The Quakers who worked to maintain neutral postures during the war became subject to persecution from both sides. Those who participated in the war in any way—whether enlisting in military service, assisting in the war effort by carting supplies or collecting blankets for the army—were disowned from the Society of Friends. Quakers who paid military fines or taxes, served in public offices, sailed on privateers or made war materials were also disowned.[33]

The events of the war clearly divided the Quakers. Families moved from Queens and Long Island to Westchester and Duchess Counties and farther north to the Finger Lakes region of New York State. When the British left New York in 1783, thirty-five thousand Loyalists left with them and moved to Canada and the West Indies. One thousand of these were Quakers from Long Island. Those pacifist Quakers who remained on Long Island had amply demonstrated their strong convictions in their religious testimonies. Committees were established to help both Quaker and African victims of the war who had been left without shelter and food. Meanwhile, the Quakers continued their efforts to free enslaved people, using their influence to foster the understanding that all men are created equal. When New York lawmakers began to consider outlawing slavery, Elias Hicks, Silas Downey, James Mott and Edmund Prior—all members of the Westbury Meeting—supported the position that slavery should be outlawed in the state.[34]

# THE FIRST FREE BLACK COMMUNITIES ON LONG ISLAND

There are many sources written about the history of enslaved people in New York and Long Island, but little is written about the development of the political landscape that forced enslaved people to escape. Finding this information offered a challenge. Endnotes can often be good sources for uncovering primary sources, and such was the case when I came to a reference marked with the name Henry Onderdonk Jr. He constructed two resources from newspaper clippings: *The Annals of Hempstead, 1643–1832* and documents that are compiled in book form in *Long Island in the Olden Times*. The *Annals* is a collection of original newspaper clippings from 1643 to 1832. The collection is held in reserve in a black cardboard box in the historical section of the New York City Public Library. Although I was forced to wait at the library for forty-five minutes for the box to arrive, I was rewarded with an opportunity to review a collection of newspaper clippings that retell numerous stories about the lives of enslaved Africans, including shocking stories involving murders, hangings and fires. I read the entire collection word for word.

I found that the events that took place in Queens County and also present-day Nassau County helped to bring enslaved Africans and persecuted Quakers to Long Island. Together, both groups suffered from political domination, thus uniting them in a mutual understanding of oppression.

Historian Graham Hodges maintained that the first enslaved person arrived in June 1613. A young man who went by the name Rodrigues was a servant to Thijs Volchertz Mossel, the captain of the vessel *Jonge Tobias*.

Mossel and his crew were exploring the North American coast, traveling north from the West Indies. The vessel traveled up the mouth of the Hudson River, stopping briefly on Manhattan Island. A dispute developed between Rodrigues and Mossel. The decision was made to leave Rodrigues behind while Mossel returned to Amsterdam to make a claim to the region. Rodrigues was given some payment for his efforts: eighty hatchets, knives, a sword and a musket. While Mossel was away in Amsterdam, a second explorer arrived: Hendrick Christiansen, on the vessel *Fortuyn*. Rodrigues met the captain and introduced himself as "a freeman" living with the Rockway Indians. Christiansen and Rodrigues negotiated a trade agreement between all parties concerned. In April of the following year, Mossel returned to find that Rodrigues had started his own trade agreement. He was outraged and a fight ensued. Rodrigues was injured, and Mossel and his crew left, again leaving him behind. Rodrigues was a man of many talents and became the father of a number of children while living out his life on Long Island. Rodrigues, who married and settled among the native Rockways, is believed to be the first African Creole and nonindigenous resident of Long Island.[35]

Twelve years later, in 1625, the Dutch West India Company took control of Manhattan Island. During this same year, pirates sold sixteen Africans to the company. These slaves had been captured from a Spanish vessel. Two years later, several African women were brought from the West Indies to New Amsterdam. These people formed the first recorded African Creole community in the colonies.[36]

By the middle of the seventeenth century, the early settlers on Long Island, along with those of the English colony Gravesend and the Dutch colony New Amsterdam, had asked the directors of the Dutch West India Company if they might bring more men as indentured servants from Europe to assist in the development of the colony. The directors in Holland felt that the cost would be too high for Europeans, who were the first enslaved workers, and suggested that the importation of slaves from Africa would better serve the purpose. They wrote in 1646, "We have seen that more Negroes could be advantageously employed and sold." This account from Henry Onderdonk Jr. dates the first slaves arriving from Africa on August 6, 1655, on the ship *Witte Paert*. This understanding included a 10 percent tax to be placed on any slave sold outside New Amsterdam.[37]

In 1660, more slaves were sent from the west coast of Africa on the ship *Eykensenboom* with orders from the directors to sell the slaves at public auction to the highest bidder, with the stipulation that they be used to help create farmland for the production of food and commodities such as flax for linen.

New York Slave Market. *Queens Historical Society.*

Later ships were sent from the West Indies and Madagascar. Enslaved people from the West Indies were preferred. Early settlers found that enslaved Creole African people were stronger, were more accustomed to hard labor and could speak English. In 1664, the last year of the Dutch occupation of New York, a law was passed for the emancipation of enslaved Africans who had "been in loyal service and had demonstrated good behavior."[38]

The need for labor to help build the settlements on Long Island is evidenced in the growth in the number of enslaved people from 1698 to just before the Revolutionary War. In 1698, there were 199 enslaved people out of a total population of 3,565. By 1700, the number of enslaved people in New York and on Long Island was greater than 15 percent of the total population. This number was larger than the number of enslaved people in the Virginia colony. In 1700, there were eight different towns on Long Island; the census of each reported the amount of enslaved people, broken down by the number of adults and children living in each town. By 1722, the census in the town of Hempstead showed a growth in the number of enslaved people, to 319. This means that there was 1 enslaved person for every 5 white people. Of the 319, 127 of the enslaved people were children. The largest number of enslaved Africans was found in Queens County, and that recorded number peaked in 1790 at 2,039.

The numbers tell us first that enslaved people were separated from their families. If there were two slaves in a residence, and the couple had a child, the child was typically sold and sent to live with another family. In some cases, married men and women lived separately. These were often arranged marriages; consequently, when a child of an enslaved African was born, the child was automatically enslaved. Enslaved children were sold and bought to be playmates for white children. There are many stories of young white children playing with young enslaved African children on Long Island. Thus, families were typically separated in some way. A change in this practice did begin to take shape during and after the Revolutionary War, when the Queens County census reported in 1790 that there were 2,039 enslaved people. Ten years later, in 1800, the number decreases to 1,528. In another ten years, the number drops to less than half, to 630 enslaved people. This is a result of the early Quaker initiative to free their slaves and thus establish free black communities. These communities then became safe places for self-emancipating blacks to come and live among free blacks.[39]

Furthermore, the Dutch West India Company brought a small group of Europeans and Africans to provide the labor to help establish the new colony. This group was indentured to either an owner or the company farms. Under this system, some had more freedom than others. Some were treated as slaves in a traditional sense, while others worked as servants and were given more freedom. According to historian Edgar McManus, the Dutch instituted a type of manumission that provided them with a "part-free" status; this allowed the Africans to purchase their own freedom in a way similar to paying off a debt. The original Creole Africans were given part-free status and property of their own. This also allowed the Dutch West India Company to have the Africans work when work was needed while allowing them freedom to support themselves. These Africans often had many of the same rights as whites. An English sea captain captured by the Dutch wrote in his diary, "Their blacks…were very free and familiar; sometimes sauntering about among the whites at meal time, with hat on head and freely joining occasionally in conversation, as if they were one and all of the same housed hold."[40]

In 1667, the English occupied New Amsterdam and renamed the colony New York. Many changes were made by the English regarding people held in bondage. It is interesting to remember that at this point in history the Dutch had freed a group of former enslaved Africans. These people started their own communities. Some intermarried with Native Americans, and some also purchased Africans as slaves themselves. There were freed Africans living in New York and in parts of Long Island by the mid-1600s.[41]

Under the English, the laws became more stringent, especially against runaway slaves, who were told that they had to be returned to their "Master or Dame." In 1683, the laws passed by an act of the province decreed that "[n]o slave could sell or give away any commodity under punishment of corporal punishment." If a slave ran away, "all Constables and Inferior Officers were herby strickly required and commanded, authorized and empowered to press, Men, Horses, boats or Primaces to pursue such prison by Sea or Land and to make diligent Hue and Cry as by law required."[42]

By 1706, though, it did not seem that these precautions had restricted the actions of the enslaved population enough. Hence, a new declaration was set by the governor of the province:

*Whereas I am informed that several negroes in this County have assemble themselves in riotous manner, which, it not prevented may prove of ill consequence; you and every one of you are therefore hereby required and commanded to take all proper methods for the seizing and apprehending of all such negroes in the said county, as shall be found to be assembled in such manner aforesaid, or have run away or absconded from their masters or owners, whereby there may be reason to suspect them ill practices or designs and to secure them in safe custody, that their crimes and actions may be inquired into; and if any of them refuse to submit themselves, then to fire on them, kill or destroy them, if they cannot otherwise be taken.*[43]

While the Quakers were settling on Long Island, the slave trade was flourishing here, with slaves being imported primarily from Guinea. Some Long Island Quakers owned slaves. They purchased African slaves from Quaker shipowners who found slavery a lucrative business. Since slaves were skilled in a variety of occupations, sales records of slaves were included in newspapers, such as in this November 15, 1762 ad in the *New York Mercury*:

*To be sold at public Vendue, tomorrow, Cruger's Wharf between 11 and 12 O'clock, on board the Sloop Rebecca and Joseph just arrived from Anambo in Guinea, a parcel of likely slaves—men and women and boys.*[44]

Some slaves were auctioned publicly on Wall Street, while others were advertised in newspapers for sale by their owners. It was the custom of some Dutch settlers to have an enslaved person find a new owner himself. The enslaved person would be sent out to perspective buyers with a letter of introduction—a note to explain the terms of the agreement. One such case appeared in the paper in Brookhaven, Long Island, recounting how a slave named Ned learned to write. He wrote his own pass and used the note to find freedom.[45]

By 1711, the enslaved population had become so numerous that a large group of enslaved people decided to rebel for their freedom. And rise up they did. Historians reported that some slaves set fire to houses and waited for their masters to return to attack them. The slave uprising was soon put down and resulted in inhuman public tortures. "Some [slaves] were broken on a wheel—a strange punishment in this hemisphere—some were burnt to death, some were cased in iron and suspended alive on gibbets where they were left to starve to death and become prey of the fowls of heaven, others were let off with simple hanging down, and what resulted were inhuman public tortures."[46]

A more comprehensive law needed to be initiated to prevent any repeat of the event. Many masters felt that too many liberties had been given to enslaved people and that they needed to institute a penalty for buying goods from Africans. In this way, an enslaved person would not have a way of earning money. This would prevent those who were enslaved from making and selling goods for their own profit. Permission was granted to any master or mistress to "punish slaves for their crimes at their discretion, not exceeding Life or Limb." It also became unlawful for more than three enslaved people to congregate because it was believed that they might be making plans to run away. The penalty for running away was that the enslaved person would be "whipped upon a naked back not to extend more than forty times." Furthermore, no one was allowed to "employ, harbor, conceal or entertain another man's slave without the consent from the slaves' master."[47]

Freed Africans who helped enslaved people were fined ten pounds for every twenty-four hours they were in their home, while whites were charged only five pounds. Enslaved people were considered the property of their masters and therefore were subject to English criminal laws. Masters were fined if their enslaved person stole or committed small crimes. However, the law was very clear that slaves could only testify in court against other slaves in cases where a slave could report on plots "to run way or kill and destroy their Master or other homes, barns, haystacks or killing cattle." It was also unlawful for enslaved people to carry firearms or clubs. Further restrictions were placed on masters who wanted to manumit their enslaved Africans to deter them from freeing them. On Long Island, each master was charged two hundred pounds for each enslaved person who was manumitted. The fee was to be given to the town as a bond so that the former enslaved person would not be a burden to others.[48] These restrictions led to another uprising in 1741.[49]

The riot was believed to have been inspired by a "Popis [Papist] priest." A series of incidents is believed to have preceded the event. Some silver and other goods were stolen by an indentured servant girl (probably European). Mary Burton, another indentured servant, was arrested for the crime and then given her freedom in exchange for information regarding the robbery. She implicated several Africans, who were then arrested. A few weeks later, the governor's house was burned to the ground, and many fires followed. Many people of New York were convinced that this was a plot. Africans were indiscriminately snatched off the street and put in jail. The white priest and his associates were hanged. Between May 11 and August 29, 154 Africans were put in prison—14 were subsequently burned at the stake, 18 were hanged and 71 were deported. Just 24 whites were imprisoned, and only 4 were executed.[50]

The residents of Long Island were terrified that the riots would continue here. Consequently, Long Island slaves were forbidden to mingle with the enslaved people in New York City. Henry Onderdonk Jr. reported that several arrests were made on Long Island. He reported an incident in which a white slave owner overheard two slaves talking about the riots: "Will said to Robin, 'What you think of Corlear's Hook or THE Plot? D—n it,' replied Robin, 'I'll have nothing to do with it or say to it if they [the slaves] will put their finger in the fire they must feel the pain; let them go on and prosper.'" Based on this very slim evidence, the Long Island slave known as Dr. Harry was hanged, and two other slaves were deported.[51]

By the mid-1700s, the severity of the laws governing slavery was increasing. After committing a misdemeanor, enslaved people were given immediate trials. Oftentimes, evidence was not presented, and enslaved people were never represented by counsel. Justices of the peace and freeholders had their own best interests in mind. Sentencing was quickly carried out. In 1772, for example, Nathaniel Brewster of Brook Haven (Brookhaven Township) "was whipping his slave who had reputably disobeyed his master. Suddenly, the slave turned and struck him." Brewster died as a result of his injuries. The enslaved man was tried the very next day by three justices of the peace and five freeholders (as the law directed) and was sentenced to death by hanging, although some of the judges felt that "the slave should be burnt or gibbeted."[52]

Some historians mentioned that enslaved people were well cared for and felt safe in their own homes. This could very well have been the case for some Africans on Long Island, yet most slave owners treated enslaved people as their property. When they feared that that their enslaved property might escape, it was not uncommon for them to brand the slave with the initials of the master. Branded initials could be seen on the arms of an enslaved person, and sometimes the enslaved person was forced to wear an iron collar around the neck.[53]

Evidence of such inhuman treatment can be found in newspaper advertisements for runaways slaves published in the *Long Island Farmer*:

£16 REWARD—Absconded from their owners
at the house of Domine Rubell at Flatbush, two
negro slaves, Betsy marked T.A. on her right
shoulder and Polly with our mark—September 1781[54]

Ran away from Jeromus Lott at Flatlands, a negro boy
named Jack, 16 years old. He had on his neck an iron
collar marked J.L. The name of his owner—May 20th 1784[55]

Advertisements for runaways are clear evidence that slaves did run away. Slaves were required to carry a pass when they were traveling alone, a practice that indicates that slaves disappeared when a chance for freedom arose: "Notice—a negro wandering about without a pass was taken up at Hempstead by Benjamin Stewart, school master, and put in jail, where he now awaits the order of his master—May 5th 1760."[56]

Historians have also noted that it was not uncommon for slaves who learned a trade to escape. Men with trades such as milling, fence building or shipbuilding—as was the case with the famous slave Frederick Douglass—were more likely to seek freedom. It was also more common for a slave who was proficient in language or could read or write to run away:[57]

> £6 REWARD Ran Away
> Hendrick Onderdonk at Cow Neck
> a negro named Primus.
> It is likely he forged a pass, for
> he can read and write—August 13, 1760[58]

The precise number of runaway slaves on Long Island is not known. Newspaper notices for runaways began to appear as soon as newspapers became regular publications in the early 1700s. From 1750 to 1770, notices for runaways were very common, and they were usually clustered in small paragraphs with a notice for a reward.[59]

Careful review of the slave ads revealed some noteworthy patterns. Jonathan Prude, in his research on slavery, created a series of tables that examined various elements of runaways recorded from different geographic areas around New York. Of importance were the escape strategies used by runaways and the origins and destinations of runaways. Prude completed an extensive review of the runaway ads that were printed in the *New York Gazette* between 1716 and 1783.[60] The top strategy employed by runaways was to pretend to be free. The second most common was to forge a pass or use an old pass.

A combination of strategies appears to have been employed by an escaping slave named Anthony, who appeared in the *New York Gazette* and the *Weekly Mercury*, no. 1673, on November 10, 1783:

> RUN-AWAY on Tuesday night the 4th instant,
> from the subscriber at Hempstead, in
> Queen's county, Long Island a negro man slave named
> ANTHONY;

*about 35 years old, of a middling stature, a black*
*complexion, very talkative, speaks good English, and*
*pretends to be a preacher, and sometimes officiates*
*in that capacity among Blacks. Had on when he went*
*away a bearskin great coat, and the rest of the cloaths*
*chiefly of the same kind, and partly worn, and may very*
*likely have changed his clothes. Any person who will*
*apprehend said negro man, and delivers him to the*
*subscriber, or secures him so that his master may have him again,*
*shall receive a reward of FIVE DOLLARS, if taken in Queens's*
*county; and TEN DOLLARS if taken elsewhere to be paid by me.*

*N.B. All masters of vessels, and others, are hereby forbid to*
*carry him off, &c. S. CLOWES.*

Another section of slave runaway ads included listings of the various stolen goods that runaways took when they left. Interestingly, traveling with another slave was top on the list, and clothing was second. In another ad, a description of the escaping slave contains no names—just the physical descriptions and clothing. The following was posted by both the *New York Gazette* and the *Weekly Post-Boy*, no. 703, on July 5, 1756:

*Run away the 2d instant July, from John Decker,*
*of Staten Island, a negro Man, being short chubby*
*fellow, with extraordinary bushy Hair, is barefoot and*
*has a Soldier's red Great Coat on Also ran away*
*from the Widow Haughwout, of said Island negro*
*wench, of Middle Size, is with child, and speaks*
*English, and has a bundle of clothes with her.*
*It is supposed they went together. Whoever takes*
*up said negro Man and Wench, and secures them so*
*that they may be had again, shall have Forty Shillings*
*Reward and Charges paid by the Owners, John Decker*
*and Widow Haughwout.*

This is an interesting ad for many reasons, but it demonstrates that separated families attempted to escape together with only a bundle of clothes.

The means of transportation came third. Boats were on the top of that list, and horses were second. Taking the master's money and other objects

An escaping slave on a raft. *Queens Historical Society.*

of value was also considered a method of escaping. The *New York Gazette* and the *Weekly Post-Boy*, no. 748, on May 16, 1757, offered this:

> *Run away the 25ᵗʰ of April last, from Thomas*
> *Robinson of Brookhaven in the County of Suffolk,*
> *on Long Island, a negro man named Ned, about*
> *23 years old, he stole a Barge and was seen on the*
> *Thursday following the Sound opposite to Lloyd's Neck,*
> *steering the Westward. The Barge has lost part of her*
> *stem and several of her Timbers broke, He has a crooked*
> *Knee. Had on when he went away a new grey Kersey*
> *Coat, a new Pair of Pumps. The said negro can both*
> *read and write, and probably has wrote himself a Pass.*
> *Whoever takes up the said negro and secures him so*
> *that his master may have him again shall have*
> *Twenty Shillings Reward and all reasonable*
> *Charges paid by Thomas Robinson, jun.*

The *New York Gazette*, revived in the *Weekly Post-Boy*, no. 338, on July 10, 1749, printed the following:

> *Runaway the 21ˢᵗ Instant from William and Benjamin*
> *Hawxshurst, of Oyster Bay, on Long Island, a Negro*

*Man named Tom, a middle size yellow Fellow, and is
pretty well cloath'd: Took with him a black Horse with
a white Snip or Spot on his Nose. Whoever takes up and
secures the said Negro and Horse, shall have a reasonable
Reward paid by William and Benjamin Hawxshurst.*

The struggles by Africans and Quakers for personal freedom during the Revolutionary War intensified their mutual understanding of oppression. At the outbreak of war in 1775, the army was composed mainly of volunteers. A new law was passed concerning the fate of all enslaved people, stating, "In case of an Alarm or actual invasion, every man holding an able man slave is to deliver him to an officer to that purpose. Every such slave to be employed at the Artillery of the fortifications."[61]

To prevent against insurrection by the slaves, they were still held to the provision of carrying a pass; they could be shot on sight if they were more than a mile from home. Slave owners who did not surrender their slaves were fined forty pounds. In the event that the slave was killed, six freeholders on the board would decide on the current value of the slave to recompense the owner. However, a slave who enlisted in the military with his master's consent was given his freedom.[62]

Why were runaways coming to Long Island? Members of the Society of Friends on Long Island had manumitted 154 slaves by the end of the Revolutionary War. Many freed blacks stayed on the farms where they had been slaves. Others were taken in as apprentices and taught trades such as making barrels and hats. In time, some families were reunited, and black communities were established again. Many such communities were founded with the assistance of the Quakers. With the establishment of free communities, runaways could come to Long Island, find work and hide among free blacks. And they did.

The following chapters will tell the stories of how the Quakers from Long Island worked to assist runaways long before the phrase "Underground Railroad" was used to define their actions. Because history is the continuous account of people and events, one act of human kindness can produce another. Some of the ideals of human equality evolved from the Quaker beliefs that all men and women are equal in the sight of God. Their strict adherence to the scriptures of the Bible helped to empower the actions taken by members of the Society of Friends. This guiding principle from Deuteronomy 23:15 helped them to take action on their beliefs: "Thou shalt not deliver unto his master the servant that has escaped from his master unto thee."

# ELIAS HICKS

## THE PROPHET FROM JERICHO

In Jericho, Long Island, Quaker minister, teacher and surveyor Elias Hicks is remembered for his moral convictions against slavery. In 1811, he wrote, "It was universally acknowledged that man was a moral agent, accountable for his personal conduct; and further, that everyman is a free agent and thus born free, no matter what the situation of his parents."[63]

Elias Hicks was born in the town of Hempstead on March 19, 1748, the son of John and Martha Smith Hicks. John became a Quaker and was a member of the Westbury Friends Meeting at the time of Elias's birth. Martha was also a member of the meeting but had some difficulties understanding the principles of quietism; even so, she was liked by many, respected for her morality and loved by her neighbors. Mary died in 1759 when Elias was a young boy. He was raised by his uncle Samuel in Far Rockaway. Elias became friends with Walt Whitman's grandfather, who allowed him to participate in dancing and horse racing. By the time he was seventeen, Elias had "lost much of his youthful innocence" and had fallen off the course of a Quaker's way of life. When his father remarried, to Phebe Powell, Elias came back to Hempstead and became a carpenter's apprentice. Soon, Elias began to miss his early spiritual background and started to spend long hours reading the Bible. Elias learned how to be a surveyor and worked in Hempstead. He then began to teach in the village school. Bliss Forbush retold that one of his pupils wrote a tribute to Elias, noting, "The manners of Elias Hicks were so mild, his deportment so dignified, and his conversation so instructive, that it left an impression for good on many of his pupils, minds that time never effaced."[64]

Elias Hicks. *Library of Congress.*

In 1771, Elias Hicks married Jemima Seaman and came to live in the Seaman home in Jericho, New York. The village of Jericho is located at the intersection of South Oyster Bay Road and Jericho Turnpike. By the mid-1700s, the turnpike connected New York City by ferry on Fulton Street through Brooklyn to the most eastern points of Long Island. Crossing north–south was the road to Oyster Bay and Massapequa. Later, Jericho Turnpike was used to haul produce in farm wagons across Queens and into New York. The village of Jericho was part of a larger tract of land purchased by Robert Williams from the Indians in 1648. The area became known as Ludsum (or the Farms) when Quakers began settling in the area as early as 1676. When Elias and Jemima came to live in Jericho, there were about twelve houses at the crossroads. The Johnathan Seaman farm contained approximately seventy-five acres. The main house was considered large for its day. There were two large rooms facing east and a long hallway leading to the wing where three slaves lived. There was a large kitchen in the rear of the house that contained a sizable brick oven. Four massive chimneys rose from the roof for the fireplaces used to heat the house.[65]

Three years after his marriage, Elias had a profound change in his outlook on life. Bliss Forbush described Elias as searching for God's grace in relation to the mistakes of his youth. He waited for a resolution as he pleaded with God, "hoping that he could experience reconciliation." At last, "light broke forth and of obscurity and [his] darkness became as the noon-day." Much strengthened by "deep openings in the visions of light," Elias was "conscious that his perplexities were resolved."[66] He was twenty-six years old and began to give more attention to the beliefs and practices of the Society of Friends.

He began to speak out at meetings and was vocal about the "great truths" manifested by George Fox. As time went on, Elias contemplated his

Exterior of the Elias Hicks House. *Velsor Collection.*

spiritual mission. He was appointed and accepted memberships to various committees. This meant that he had to attend First and Fourth-day Meetings for Worship in Jericho and Preparative and Monthly Meetings for Business at Westbury. It also meant the acceptance of an occasional appointment as a representative to the Quarterly Meeting. In 1773, the Yearly Meeting was held in Flushing, and Elias was invited to attend.[67]

# ELIAS HICKS'S TESTIMONY AGAINST SLAVERY

By 1773, the slave population ratio on Long Island had grown to one slave for every five settlers. The members of the Yearly Meeting in Flushing took a firmer stand in urging members not to purchase enslaved people. Elias Hicks attended that meeting. Elias was confronted with the issue of slavery. His father-in-law owned three slaves, and therefore Elias met head-on with his own views of slavery. Searching for the right response, he stood in the meeting and reminded members that the Quaker community would disown anyone who continued to buy or sell slaves or did not free those who came of age of eighteen or twenty-one, according to their sex, or if their posterity was kept in bondage.[68]

This prompted others to take action. The Yearly Meeting directed other meetings to appoint committees to visit "all in profession with [Friends] who hold Negroes to restore them their natural rights to Liberty as soon as they arrive at a suitable age for freedom." At this moment, Elias accepted his first responsibility to combat slavery.[69] Accepting his calling, he traveled with his fellow committee members to farms across Queens County only to discover that many slave owners were not willing to free and educate their slaves. Elias struggled with the issues and by the end of the first year found that more and more Friends were willing to educate and to manumit their slaves.

Between 1775 and 1776, eighty-five enslaved people were freed by owners on Long Island by the members of the Westbury Meeting. Among these owners was Elias's father, John Hicks, who freed his slave Tom Leenor, with whom Elias had played as a boy. Charles and six other minors also received their manumission papers, intended to take effect when they reached the proper age. Elias's brother, Samuel, also agreed to free his slave. The Seaman family, Elias's in-laws, freed three slaves. The first was Ben, who was given his freedom; two other slaves remained with the Seaman family and were paid for their service.[70] Later that year, the Westbury Friends Meeting appointed Elias Hicks and Gideon Seaman to meet with those Quaker families who still had enslaved people to discuss their manumission. Through their efforts alone, 154 manumissions were recorded by 1791 in Queens County.[71] Among the manumissions were those recorded by members Samuel Willis, Phebe Willets Mott Dodge and Ester (Williams) Seaman.[72]

Throughout his life, Elias Hicks expressed his strong concern for the welfare of enslaved people and former enslaved people. More importantly, he continually acted on his convictions, including his belief that those who had benefited from slavery were responsible for educating former enslaved adults and their children. He was the driving force behind the formation of the Charity Society on June 7, 1794, by thirty members of the Jericho and Westbury Friends Meetings. The Charity Society's mission was to "help improve the poor among the African people by educating their children."

Efforts to educate the children began slowly. Former enslaved children and Quaker children were originally taught in Quaker homes in Jericho. In 1817, the Westbury and Jericho Meetings appointed Elias Hicks and Gideon Seaman to visit the families of potential students, children and adults, to encourage them to promote education. African parents said that they would be more willing to let their children attend school in their own neighborhoods rather then take them to Quaker homes. Consequently, at the insistence of Elias Hicks, three schools were opened in African neighborhoods. School was held on the First Day (Sunday), after religious services. People of all ages, even adults, were encouraged to attend. One of the schools was opened by the Charity Society on April 27, 1817, in the Westbury neighborhood then known as Guinea (present-day Glen Cove Road and the Long Island Expressway). The school served as both a primary school and a Sunday school.[73]

# Elias Hicks's Ministry, 1778–1829

Elias Hicks began his ministry in 1778. He was appointed to the Preparative Meeting of Ministers and Elders. As a recorded preacher in the Society of Friends, he dedicated himself to spreading the word of the gospel. His contribution to the development of the Underground Railroad came from his willingness to address the issues of slavery. He acted on the belief that all men are equal in the sight of God. He maintained an active ministry, traveling from Long Island to meet with other Quaker and non-Quaker communities to preach against slavery. He traveled throughout New York State and New England and then south through New Jersey, Maryland, Pennsylvania, Ohio and Indiana.

According to Hugh Barbour, Elias Hicks used his ministry to speak out against slavery whenever and wherever the opportunity arose. Hicks preached the doctrine that God's work within human hearts is in proportion to the stilling of self-will, also known as quietism.[74] As a quietist, he believed that God could speak directly to anyone, regardless of gender, race or age. If one accepts the idea that God speaks directly to anyone, it follows that slaves should be freed. It then also follows that they should be educated. At the Yearly Meeting in the spring of 1810, a new revision of the Friends Discipline was approved, ignoring a previous query cautioning Friends against dealing in prize goods.[75] The New York Friends felt that they could not distinguish any longer goods produced by slaves or free labor.

Outraged, Elias returned to Jericho and wrote an essay that condemned slavery almost as vigorously as any that had ever come from a Quaker pen.[76]

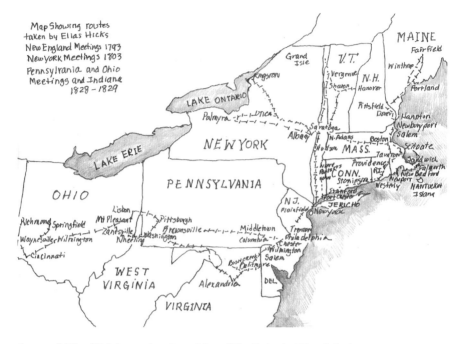

A map of Elias Hicks's travels, adopted from Bliss Forbush. *Velsor Collection.*

Hicks published the twenty-four-page pamphlet in 1811. The title page was as follows:

*OBSERVATIONS*
*ON THE*
*SLAVERY OF AFRICANS*
*AND*
*THEIR DESCENDANTS*
*Recommended to the Serious Perusal, and*
*Impartial Consideration of the Citizens of the United States*
*of America, and others concerned*

Below his name were two verses from the Bible:

*Open thy mouth for the dumb in the cause of all such*
*as are appointed for destruction.*
*Open thy mouth, judge righteously, and plead the*
*cause of the poor and needy.*
*Proverbs XXXI, 8, 9.*

Aimed at Quakers and non-Quakers alike, the pamphlet detailed his observations on slavery in a series of nineteen queries about this institution. Hicks believed quite strongly that individuals were responsible for their own actions. Hicks acknowledged that since slavery was such a long-established institution, custom deluded even profoundly committed Christians into thinking that slavery was neither an injustice nor an inequity. Noting further that liberty was Americans' most prized possession, he invited people to examine the foundations on which slavery had been built and questioned how they could possibly be in concert with the American ideal of freedom. Divine guidance, he thought, made it clear that slaves should be considered a product of war; thus, enslavement robbed its victims of liberty. To buy a slave was to become an accessory to the theft of liberty. Likewise, all products produced by the forced labor of slaves would make the buyers of those products participants in slavery.

After writing the queries with the appropriate responses, Elias Hicks punctuated his comments with a scenario: "Suppose the way for obtaining slaves from Africa was entirely intercepted, and no other place opened for obtaining any except in the rivers of the Delaware and Hudson...that the slave traders were continually infesting the shores of those rivers; that they frequently kidnapped, and sometimes by force carried off inhabitants to the West Indies, and sold them as slaves." He described the slave traders coming to the homes of Quakers, burning towns and carrying men and women and children away chained together like cattle. Men were separated from the wives they loved, and their children were sold. Elias then described the white slaves driven like swine and herded to the market to be sold and branded with a red-hot iron. Elias concluded his writing with a pronouncement:

> *Is it possible there should be...a man with a heart so hard as to assent to purchase, and make use of the fruit of the labour of his fellow citizens, his kindred and friends, produced in the horrid manner above stated, and taken from them by the unjust hand of cruelty and oppressive force? Would not every sympathetic heart, at the sight of a piece of sugar, or other produce... be filled with anguish...Would not consider the individual who would dare to be so hardy as to traffic in and use the produce of such labour...the open and avowed enemy of both God and man?*[77]

Elias Hicks wrote *Observations* sitting at his desk in his home in Jericho nearly twenty years before William Lloyd Garrison took up his campaign to abolish slavery. Bliss Forbush suggested that the seeds for Garrison's ideas were first written here and later used to start the abolition crusade. The Meeting for Suffering approved the publication, and in the preface of the second printing, Elias added his expressed belief that even if a man should write that he has the right to enslave another, the title to the slave was invalidated because such action was a criminal offense in the sight of God.[78]

Many Friends joined the campaign against products made by enslaved people. Products such as cotton, sugar, coffee and rice were on a list that many followers found to be a good outlet for antislavery sentiments. James Mott, husband of Lucretia Coffin Mott,[79] endorsed this practice and limited his family to maple sugar. He always wore linen and never allowed rice in his house. The writing of *Observations* set Elias apart as a notable friend and benefactor of the enslaved people.[80]

# ELIAS HICKS: HICKSITE FOLLOWERS

By 1811, the Society of Friends had entered into a period of crisis. There was a conflict in the annual "Epistle" sent by Friends in England. Several doctrines were being preached in the New York Yearly Meeting, and some Quakers felt that there was a need to follow a definite or "Orthodox" creed. Elias Hicks spoke out against this idea with great passion. Hicks's followers were called Hicksites.[81] They strongly interpreted the doctrine of the Inner Light to mean that they were responsible for taking action whenever necessary. Given the testimony of equality that Hicks believed was God-given, the issue of slavery had to be confronted. Hicksites felt compelled to act to see that slavery was ended within their lifetimes. In this way, Elias Hicks's followers set the standard for antislavery sentiment, first in Jericho and Long Island and then at Philadelphia and Baltimore Meetings. This sentiment meant taking action, such as assisting runaways to safety by way of the Underground Railroad. Of the 223 members of the Jericho Meeting, 211 sided with Hicks, 9 withdrew and 3 remained neutral. In New York, Philadelphia and Baltimore Meetings, the Hicksites were the majority, but the Ohio Meeting was equally divided. Hicks's principles took root within his followers and their testimonies, and by their actions. Hicksite Quakers set examples that helped to create the abolitionist movement in the United States.[82]

In 1824, Elias Hicks delivered a sermon that explicitly spoke out against racial prejudice:

*We are on the level with all the rest of God's creatures. We are not better for being white, than others for being black; and we have no more right to oppress the blacks because they are black than they have to oppress us because we are white. Can God oppress? Has He not as good a right to look upon whites as inferior as we look upon black Oh! That we might rise above it!*[83]

In 1825, Elias Hicks wrote *A Series of Extemporaneous Discourses*, from which the following was taken:

*I can look back and remember well, when one among my brethren, I laboured to put an end to this slavery; and what hard work it was to convince the aged. How unwilling they were to comply with anything but that which they had been long inured to, and which had become to them like second nature. They looked back and saw, that good men before them had done the same thing; and, said they, shall we think to be better than they were. This was for want of considering, that such was the darkness of the children of men, that no one generation has arrived at perfection. There is as much to be done in each generation, as has been done by the one which preceded it: because in the same proportion as we advance in reformation, the way is open for greater advancement. The primitive disciples were far from a state of perfection, otherwise an apostasy could not have entered. They were brought out of darkness, as far as their case would admit. So with our primitive Friends, they did their day's work faithfully; but how far short did they come! Therefore, if we rest in their labours we are going back; for every generation has a work to do, in addition to the previous one. If we do nothing more, we spend our time in vain.*[84]

Elias Hicks died in 1830. The memorial written in honor of him is very moving. A statement issued by the African Benevolent Societies of New York referred to his "indefatigable exertions against slavery, [his] purity of life, sincerity of profession, [and] active exertion in the cause of human improvement. Few men can bear comparison with this friend on humanity."

The impact Elias Hicks had on the Quaker communities associated with the Jericho and other Long Island Meetings is significant. The growth of antislavery sentiment among Quakers was grounded in a belief in the Inner Light and in a conviction regarding man's ability to choose his own salvation. Believing and espousing these principles made Elias Hicks not just a prophet but also a "Friend" of humanity.[85]

The practice of helping slaves run to freedom began not by political action but rather from a shared understanding of oppression and the Quakers' strong conviction that all men are equal in the sight of God and that God can speak to anyone regardless of race, gender or age. Jericho's Hicksite Quakers' testimonies against slavery allowed other Quakers to take action.

Their actions, recorded in the Westbury and Jericho Meetings, included the early manumission of any slaves held by Quakers, purchasing slaves for the express purpose of freeing them, assisting in the creation of free black communities, fostering the creation of the Charity Society for building schools to educate African-descended children, supporting the free produce movement, assisting runaway slaves to safety and providing a safe place to stay until a new location could be found.

In addition, due in part to Elias Hicks's efforts, the State of New York abolished slavery on July 4, 1827. Hicksite Quakers participated in these activities. Thus, it should be clear that they were a particularly strong force in the rise of a national abolitionist movement and the growth and advancement of the Underground Railroad.

# QUAKER FAMILIES AND
# THEIR CONNECTIONS

The challenges that early Quakers faced from non-Quaker groups only strengthened their conviction that marriages should be confined within the Society of Friends. Quakers who married out of the faith could be disowned or removed from the Society of Friends. As a result, Quaker families that settled in Cowneck (Sands Point), Jerusalem (Wantagh and North Bellmore), Jericho, Westbury, New York City and Westchester County soon developed more ties through marriage. These were in addition to those forged through purely religious convictions. These intermarried Quakers produced a powerful multigenerational force against slavery. Kinship and shared family histories, along with strong religious and cultural values, served to form networks of Hicksite Quakers in which shared social beliefs could be acted on. Paths taken by runaways generally followed routes that mirrored these familial connections.

In 1830, members of many meetings decided to become Hicksites. The routes for the Underground Railroad followed these meetinghouses—across the Long Island Sound at the Purchase Meeting in Duchess County, the Quaker Hill Meeting and Cornwall Meeting. In Connecticut, the Stanford Meeting was Hicksite. In Westchester County the Hicksite meetings were Chappaqua Meeting, the Amawalk Meeting, the Scarsdale Meeting and the Mamaroneck Meeting just to name a few. This relationship, or "road to freedom," can also be seen through the connections made by early freedom seekers who followed Quaker families

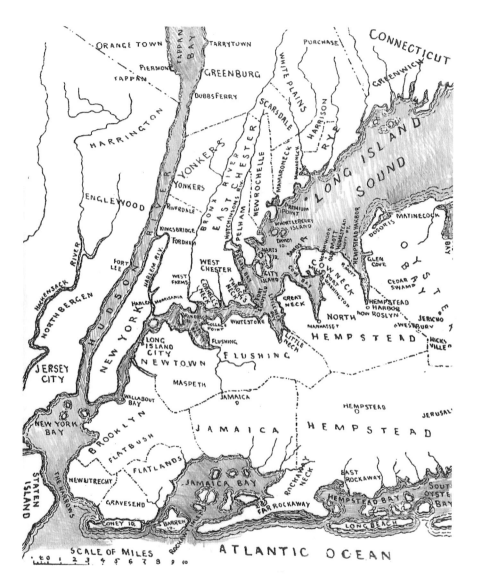

An 1890 map of Long Island. *Thomas Cornell.*

from one family member to the next and from one meetinghouse to the next. By 1850, many of these Quaker families had become extensively related and so united in their testimonies that antislavery sentiment had developed into a way of life.[86]

# THE MOTT FAMILY

One of the oldest recorded families is the Adam Mott family from Cowneck (present-day Sands Point). One of the first references that I found when researching the Underground Railroad was a book compiled in 1890 by Thomas Cornell. The book was written for the many generations of Mott families who are descendants of Adam and Anne Mott. Cornell compiled an extensive genealogy of the Quaker families who intermarried and formed the network for freedom seekers. This is an amazing story of families who formed many contacts on Long Island and in Westchester and New York City.

The original home was built in 1715 by Adam Mott. He purchased 260 acres of land from his brother, Richbell Mott. Adam Mott was a member of the Westbury Meeting. When he was sixty years old, he married Phebe Willets, who at the time was thirty-two years old and a minister in the Society of Friends. They had three children: Elizabeth, Stephen and Adam, the last of whom was born in 1734. Within six years time, father Adam died, leaving "a handsome dowry" to Elizabeth and provisions for the property to be divided between sons Stephen and Adam. The children were very young, so a stipulation was made that Phebe could stay and raise the children until Stephen was twenty-one years old. If she remarried, she needed to stay with her children but was not allowed to change any of the features of the land.

Four years later, Phebe Willets Mott married Tristram Dodge of Cow Bay. As was stipulated in the will, Tristram Dodge, a widower himself, and his son came to live at the Mott homestead. Phebe lived there for more than twenty years, raising her children and then helping to raise her grandchildren.[87] During this time, she continued her ministry, traveling to Quaker communities in New Jersey and England. She spoke out against slavery. In 1775, she was the first woman on Long Island to manumit her slave, Rachael. When Phebe returned from England in 1777, two of her children were married. Elizabeth married John Willis, and Adam married John Willis's sister, Sarah, both Quakers from Jericho.

Adam stayed in the Mott home. His brother, Stephen, built another home on the eastern side of the property. Adam Mott (a third) was born to Adam and Sarah Willis Mott in 1762 in the same rural Quaker home where his father was born. The homestead was a two-story shingled house, situated on a point overlooking the Long Island Sound and Hempstead Harbor. The waterways were their major means of transportation, for there were few highways maintained in Cowneck in those days. Many people used gated

The Old Mott Homestead. *Thomas Cornell.*

roads, private lanes and rights-of-way to make their way to Friends homes or to the Westbury Meeting.

In 1768, Adam Mott, when he was only six years old, fell in love with his remote cousin Anne Mott. Thomas Cornell wrote, "From his father's house in Cowneck shore, he could see across the sound 5 or 6 miles to the northwest, on the shores of Mamaroneck, almost in front of the little village of New Rochelle. This was the original home of James Mott, the grandson of his own grand uncle Richbell Mott."[88] James Mott's family came from New York City. They were very prosperous merchants. With the onset of the Revolutionary War, James's wife wanted to move back to be with her parents, Samuel and Ann Carpenter Underhill, in Mamaroneck. At her insistence, James purchased a home from his brother-in-law at Premium Point Mill, nestled on seventy acres on the Long Island Sound.

James Mott was a prominent member of the Society of Friends for more than fifty years. He was the clerk of the Purchase Monthly Meeting. He was often called on to travel with Elias Hicks in his ministry. James Mott was very outspoken about the advancement of education and religion and in the suppression of slavery. He spoke out against the use of products made by enslaved people. He fully supported the work of Elias Hicks, limiting his family to maple sugar, and unless they could get coffee free from the taint of slavery, they made it from peas. He always wore linen and never cotton. James's wife died at the age of thirty-two and left James with four children to raise. James's daughter Anne Mott remembered many stories of the events that took place at her home during the Revolutionary War. Her son, Richard, wrote about these stories. One story tells of the relationship between two former slaves, Billy and Jinny:

> *Prominent among the characters from whom these reminiscences were derived loom up "Uncle Billy and Aunt Jinny." I can hardly recall the time when I did not know them. She was never known as Jennie—it was always Jinny. They were old people—how old, I can only conjecture. My grandfather, then upwards of seventy, they seemed to look upon in a respectfully patronizing way, as a somewhat youthful member who became so by marrying into the family they had faithfully served through three generations. She once told of the narrow escape of one of the little boys from drowning a long time before. I found on inquiry that the little boy was my grand-uncle. Jinny was a native African, black as anthracite. Stolen when a child, but old enough to remember much of her young life. She liked to have us understand that her father was a king, or a chief, or somebody of consequence and that her young African life was free and happy—no frost, no ice, no snow there but summer all the time—without care and without clothes. Of the latter she had no experience till she was offered for sale in New York.*[89]

Billy was born in 1738. He was the son of Tom and Caty, who were the slaves of Thomas Bowne of Long Island. Jinny arrived on a slave ship in 1744, and she was bought by Samuel Underhill, the grandfather of Anne Mott, for his wife, Ann Carpenter Underhill. Jinny was brought to their home at Cedar Swamp (near Jericho) to care for their daughter, Mary Underhill. Billy was purchased and lived at a farm next door to the Underhills. Billy and Jinny married. They raised nine sons and one daughter. In 1768, Samuel Underhill moved to Mamaroneck. Samuel exchanged one of his female slaves for Billy so that the married couple could stay together. Billy and Jinny had their own home on the property and entertained many children with their stories about the Revolutionary War. Billy was a sailor and often traveled back and forth across the sound to the Mott homestead in Sands Point. In 1780, Ann Carpenter Underhill came to live with the Mott family with her grandchildren. Jinny died in 1818 and Billy in 1826.[90]

Anne and Adam Mott married in 1785 at the Purchase Meeting. Anne was seventeen years old when she came to Cowneck and lived with her in-laws. Adam soon built their own home and mill on the west side of the property in Cowbay. They became very involved in the Westbury Meeting and were followers of Elias Hicks. Anne Mott's father, James Mott, traveled extensively with Elias throughout New England and upstate New York. James was very interested in having Anne's brothers, Richard and James, continue with their education. Originally, James established a school on the property at Premium Point. He was involved in the development of the Nine Partners School near Quaker Hill in Dutchess County, New York. His son James attended that school and then was a teacher there. Many students from Long Island attended the Nine Partners School. Elias Hicks's daughters attended the school. Joseph Post and Lucretia Coffin attended the school. Lucretia was the daughter of Thomas Coffin and Anna Folger, from Nantucket. She was thirteen years old when she started at the Nine Partners School and fell in love with her English teacher, James Mott. James and Lucretia were married in 1811 at the Pine Street Meeting in Philadelphia.

Elias Hicks's ministry brought Quakers together through religious convictions, education and moral actions. Elias Hicks's firm belief from John 1:9, that "the true Light, which lighteth every man that cometh into the world," provided the foundation for early Quakers to see that all men are created equally. These convictions helped to form a multigenerational network of Quakers who actively fought against slavery. Taking action based on their beliefs was imperative to living a moral life. The following stories will demonstrate some of the paths these connected families worked to establish.

# JERUSALEM

When the phone rang, the caller explained to me that as a young girl she remembered an article in the *Daily News* that related information about the Underground Railroad in Wantagh, New York. I believe the following is the article in question. This question-and-answer article appeared in the *Daily News*, the local paper, in 1967, and it is now part of the historical collection in the Wantagh library. This is the question:

> *I'm a member of the Henry Morrison–DeLoney Post of the American Legion in Freeport. I have heard that somewhere in the Bellmore area there is a Negro cemetery where soldiers who fought in the Civil War are buried. I understand this cemetery is neglected and overgrown with weeds. Can you give me its location and tell me if it is a military burial ground. The members of our post would like to clean it up and see that it is cared for in the future. D.H., West Hempstead*

This is the response:

> *The cemetery is on Oakfield Ave. in North Bellmore near the Wantagh border. It has been neglected and is almost hidden behind trees. Headstones show that all but one of those buried there were in the Civil War. The last burial [on] record was 1943. The land was once part of the Jackson farm, so named after the leader of an abolitionist group. The Jacksons provided a link in the Underground Railroad that helped slaves escape from*

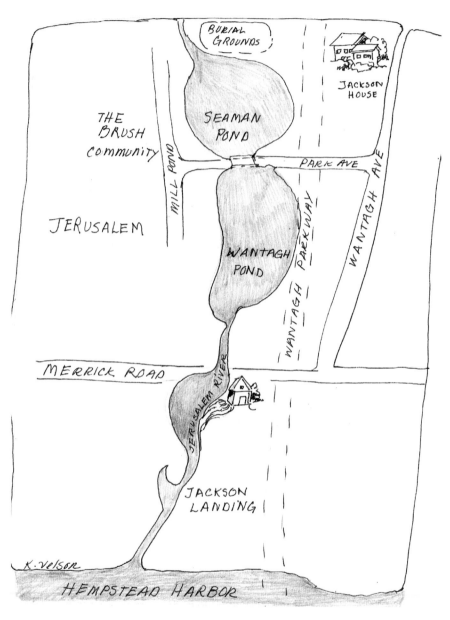

A map of Jerusalem. *Velsor Collection.*

*the South before the Civil War. The family gave several parcels of land to ex-slaves, many of whom adopted the name Jackson as the cemetery's headstones testify.*

The Jackson family was one of the first families to settle on the southwestern shore of Long Island.[91] Family records were obtained through various sources and from copies of wills. One account, compiled by J. Percey of Crayon, New Jersey, in 1902, noted that

*Robert Jackson came from Watertown Mass., to Weatherfield Conn, to Hartford, and from there to Hempstead, Long Island in 1643. This is believed to be one of the first English settlements in the western part of Long Island. His wife was Agnes Washburn. They had four children John, Samuel, Sarah and Martha. Their son John married Elizabeth Hallett. When she died he married Elizabeth Seaman. On October 9, 1684, Lieut. John Jackson went to New York to obtain a patient for the Town. April 5, 1687 Capt. Jackson went to New York to obtain a grant for 200 acres of land. In 1698 Major Jackson was granted the privilege of the Jerusalem river to set up a mill. He was afterwards Colonel and Judge of [the] Court. He left three sons Samuel, John, and James and five daughters whose names are not recorded…Samuel inherited the home at Jerusalem. John Jr. also settled at Jerusalem and died there in 1744.[92]*

The Jackson homesite. *Velsor Collection.*

John Jackson Jr. worked at the lumber mill on the Jerusalem River, which today is called the North Bellmore Creek. Jerusalem is present-day Wantagh and North Bellmore. John Jr. married Elizabeth Hallet from Oyster Bay. They joined the Society of Friends, and as was common in those days, the rest of the family followed his lead and became Quakers also. They also had a son, John, who married Thesia Mott from Great Neck. John and Thesia, too, had a son, John (born in 1733), whose second marriage was to Margaret Townsend from Oyster Bay. John and Margaret's third son was Obadiah. In 1804, Obadiah married his second wife, Rachel Underhill, and lived in Jericho. These early marriages helped to form a multigenerational tie to the Underground Railroad. These ties started first in Jerusalem, beginning in 1775 and 1776, and then persisted in Jericho and Old Westbury until after the Civil War.[93]

Economic and social growth developed rapidly in the mid- to late 1700s in Jerusalem. Active abolitionists like their forebears, the Jacksons helped to establish a free black community known as the Brush. The property was surrounded by dense vegetation of shrub oaks and pines on the west side of the Jerusalem River. During the years between 1775 and about 1865, many of those former enslaved people helped to shelter runaways coming from New York City. This established community helped many to find jobs working at the Jackson Mill.[94]

One well-used New York City freedom route had a stop in White Pot, in Newtown Township, at the home of Jarvis Jackson. Jarvis Jackson was born in Bethpage on April 17, 1781. He married Mary Whitson in 1804. They were Quakers and purchased a farm in White Pot (now Forrest Hills) on June 8, 1818. Thirty years later, he purchased an adjacent farm and doubled his holdings to 111 acres. Jarvis became a successful farmer and was prominent in his community. He was the supervisor of the town of Newtown, assessor and overseer of the poor. He became the commissioner of the local schools from 1834 to 1836. His son, George Jackson, was born in 1814 and married Elizabeth Underhill in 1838. Elizabeth and George met at the Quarterly and Yearly Meetings held at the Flushing Meetinghouse. Elizabeth's family was from Hudson, New York, a small town close to Quaker Hill. They lived on the newly acquired farm located on Flushing Creek.

A story was told by their daughter, Hannah Jackson, who was born in 1847. When she was young, she was not permitted to play in the woods above the creek. It wasn't until she was older that she learned that the woods had been a station on the Underground Railroad. Guides from

An old map of Wantagh. *Wantagh Public Library.*

New York and Brooklyn would bring escaping slaves to the woods to hide during the day, and her parents feared that she might inadvertently give away their hiding places. At night, under cover of darkness, small boats traveled down Flushing Creek to the farm where the runaways boarded. Laden with their human cargo, the boats either traveled out of Flushing Creek to Westchester County, where the connections could be made with other Quaker Meetings, or were taken to another destination, the Brush.[95]

As the numbers of runaway slaves increased, the Quaker and free black communities first settled by the Jackson family had become so well established that logic alone would have made it a regular destination on the Underground Railroad route that came through Flushing, through the waterways and byways to the Brush and ended at the old Jackson farm. Not only was this black community in a position to help runaways financially, but it also provided a place for runaways to "hide in plain sight" among a larger community of local blacks.

By the period just before the Civil War, the Jerusalem community of freed blacks and Quakers had become quite strong. In 1835, Thomas Jackson—a

The Old Burial Grounds. *Velsor Collection.*

direct descendant of John
Jackson (son of Pannenas
and Charity Coles Jackson)—
gave a parcel of land west of
Oakfield and north Bethpage
Avenues to build an African
Free School. By 1851, the
community had established an
African Methodist Episcopal
Zion Church, located north
of the schoolhouse on the
east side of Oakfield Avenue.
Forty-seven members made up
the first congregation.[96]

Next to the church was a
cemetery. Known as the Old
Burial Grounds, the sign still
holds the stories of the self-
emancipated people, as well as
the stories of the free blacks.
The sign reads, "An A.M.E.

The Jackson headstone. *Velsor Collection.*

Zion Church stood on these grounds in the nineteenth century. Interred
here are U.S. black troops from the Civil War as well as other descendents of
slaves from this area which was once called the Brush."

There are documented stories of men who were free and worked in various
occupations before enlisting in the Civil War. Some of these men returned and
are interred here. David Jackson's stone is still in the cemetery. His regiment is
listed as "I.2G. US Col troops." Jackson died in 1903 at the age of sixty-seven.
His regiment fought in sieges in Petersburg and Richmond, as well as in the
Carolinas. He completed his line of duty on September 21, 1865. He was not
healthy after the war but was remembered as a hardworking member of the
community. Three other gravestones remain: Edward Jackson, Morris Jackson
and Gilbert Jackson. They all served in the Tenth Regiment in the U.S. Colored
Troops. The Tenth Regiment served in Louisiana, Texas and Florida. The men
finished their duty in October 1865.

Edward S. Jackson was born in 1825 in the Brush. He was the son of
Morris and Percilla Jackson. He was a farmworker and enlisted as a private
on December 11, 1863. When he returned, he had six children, whom
he listed on his pension application. Three children were born before the

Civil War and three after. Morris Jackson was born in 1841 and worked as a laborer before enlisting. He was discharged as a corporal. He had five children. Gilbert Jackson was born in 1845 in Wantagh and was a farmer before he enlisted in the war. He was a private when he returned and married Martha Aurelia in 1870. They had two children before she died in 1916.[97]

The Old Burial Grounds gives clear evidence that the Brush was home to many black families, who found the Jacksons' community to be a destination point rather than a stopping point on the Underground Railroad. The Old Burial Grounds tells the story and thus stands as a tribute to those men who gave their lives to help other enslaved people be free.

# JERICHO

The hamlet of Jericho played a different role in the Underground Railroad than Jerusalem. In most cases, the Brush was considered a destination for runways, whereas Jericho over the years became an important station for securing the health and safety of enslaved people.[98] Many families in Jericho helped enslaved people to freedom. Valentine Hicks, the son-in-law of Elias Hicks, is believed by historians to have been in charge of this section on Long Island.[99]

## VALENTINE AND ABIGAIL HICKS

Valentine Hicks was a direct descendant of the Hicks family from Old Westbury. The fourth and youngest son of Samuel and Phebe Seaman Hicks, his brother was Isaac Hicks. Valentine was born in Old Westbury on April 2, 1782. He spent his childhood at the family farm. Isaac was a very successful merchant in New York City. When Valentine came of age, he was encouraged to join his brother's business and left Long Island. He became very successful and maintained his connection to Long Island and the Society of Friends. This may have been why he asked Abigail Hicks, his second cousin, to marry him. Abigail was the daughter of Elias Hicks. Together they had five children: Phebe (born in 1804), Mary (born in 1806

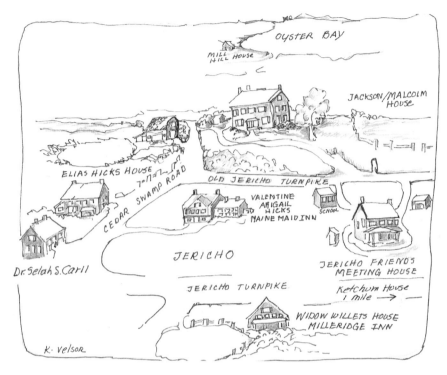

A map of Jericho. *Velsor Collection.*

and died before she was twenty years old), Caroline (born in 1808 and married Dr. William Seaman), Elizabeth (died before she was eight years old) and their only son, Elias, born in 1815 in Jericho. Like his father, he married his cousin, Sarah Hicks, who was the daughter of Robert and Mary Underhill Hicks.[100]

While Valentine was a resident in New York City, he made a major contribution to the welfare of all children. He worked to organize the Society for Establishing a Free School, a group that started the New York City Public Schools. Through his work with the Manumission Society, Valentine helped to establish a series of African Free Schools. By the time Valentine was thirty-one years old, he had accumulated $50,000 and decided to retire to Long Island.[101] In 1815, two years after the family returned to Jericho, Valentine and Abigail were able to purchase the house diagonally across the street from Elias on Old Jericho Turnpike. The house was built by Timothy Treadwell in 1789.

Originally, the house had a side hall entrance. Valentine and Abigail wanted the door to be in the center of the house, with a grand staircase

*Right*: Valentine Hicks. *Nassau County Historical Collection.*

*Below*: The Valentine and Abigail Hicks Home. *Jericho Public Library.*

wrapping around the main entrance. The renovations were completed over a period of time. Workmen were often seen at the house working on the elaborate moldings and floors. This is further evidenced by the changes that were made to the second-floor stairs and the addition of the front rooms facing the turnpike. The original floors were so well made that they are still used in the front rooms today.[102]

The home was originally on an acre of land, and over the thirty-five years they lived in Jericho, Valentine acquired eighteen more acres. Elias and Valentine Hicks's combined properties encompassed most of the property surrounding the hamlet of Jericho. When Abigail inherited property from her father in 1830, Valentine purchased Abigail's sister's shares, totaling thirty-five more acres, and they owned much of present-day Hicksville.[103]

Valentine and Abigail Hicks's house at present is the Maine Maid Inn, which was a stop on the Underground Railroad. Stories handed down through generations in the Hicks family retell how Valentine Hicks assisted fugitive slaves. One documented story is about an officially enslaved man who was working among freed blacks on the Hicks farm in Jericho when a slave catcher came to reclaim him. The slave catcher arrived by stagecoach at the tavern south of Elias Hicks's house. Valentine Hicks saw the enslaved man as he was running away from the slave catcher and stopped him,

The Maine Maid Inn. *Velsor Collection.*

opening the door to Elias Hicks's home and letting the man in. He stayed in the attic until it was safe, and he was then brought to "the bay" by wagon.[104]

After reading this story, I wondered if there were more recorded incidents of Valentine Hicks assisting escaping slaves. On a cold February afternoon, I was sitting at my desk at SUNY–Old Westbury when the phone rang. I answered the ring and identified myself. I heard a soft, deep voice; it was Leon Rushmore, a senior member of the Westbury Meeting. He invited me to lunch at the Maine Maid Inn. I accepted. Over lunch, we talked about my husband's family, who were originally members of the Westbury Friends Meeting. We shared similar interests, and he was very eager to tell me that his mother grew up in the Maine Maid Inn when it was still a private home. Leon was a descendant of Elias and Valentine Hicks. He told me the story about the escaping slave one more time, and then he explained to me that it was the custom in Jericho, many years ago, for farmers to hide their belongings from the tax collectors. The collectors were seeking money to pay to the local ministers who represented the Church of England. To avoid having the tax collectors take their possessions in lieu of payment, the Quakers built secret closets to hide their valuables. The Jericho farmers grew flax and made it into

The staircase at the Maine Maid Inn. *Thomas Abbey.*

linen. Linen was one of the sources of income for the Valentine Hicks family. Leon explained to me that runaway slaves were taken up the stairs of Valentine Hicks's home to the secret linen closet.[105]

Leon then led me up the grand staircase in the Maine Maid Inn and showed me the door to the linen closet. As he opened the door with a tug, a cold blast of air came down the stairs. With total amazement, I saw a staircase starting about three feet off the floor, making its way to the attic. He explained to me that when it was a secret closet, there were removable shelves in front of the stairs. Behind the shelves was the stair that took runaway slaves to the attic. Eight years later, I received an e-mail from a former teacher from the Locust Valley Friends School who had read about my research. Doris Pallet wrote that she often took students to the Maine Maid Inn to tell the story of the Hicks family and to see the secret stairs:

> *The linen closet had a panel immediately as you opened it…At the time it was shown to me, the panel could be pulled forward and taken out in one unit as one would unload a layered box, upright. Then the entire panel could be pressed back into the recess provided for it and the hinged door closed on it. The stair was behind all this.*

The door to the secret stair. *Thomas Abbey.*

It is very clear to me that the closet was kept as a hiding place to remind family members to retell the story the Hicks family has told and retold so many times before. I have learned since this time that there were many enslaved people, both individuals and families, who came to Jericho seeking freedom. The first runways were escaping from slavery in New York State until 1827, when slaves were freed in that state. The second wave of activity came from the connections with the Manumission Society, an organization established by Quakers and non-Quakers to help assist people to freedom. Valentine was an important community member in the city of New York and on Long Island. His work within the Society of Friends helped to make the connections to other members who would help enslaved people to freedom. As a wealthy landowner, he had the time and the means to assist in this effort. His wife, Abigail, kept the runaways in her home, giving them a place to stay and food to eat. Initially, a request for assistance was sent by courier to the New York Meeting of which Valentine and Abigail were members. Accepting the request for shelter meant taking on the responsibility for the health and safety of the enslaved people. Depending on the circumstances, connections were again made by courier for the next connection.[106]

# THE ELIAS HICKS HOUSE

The Elias Hicks House was also a place where runaways were hidden from slave catchers. This home was built by Jonathan Seaman between 1730 and 1740. The Seaman family was one of the original Quaker families to settle in Jericho. The original house was a three-story home, with a kitchen, a dining room and a parlor on the first floor and bedrooms on the second and third floors.

The house is currently owned by the County of Nassau and is rented out to a nonprofit organization. I have visited the home on a number of occasions. It is in good condition, and the former dining room is reported to be in the same condition as it would have been when Elias lived there. On the eastern wall, there is a fireplace with nice moldings and a small closet for storage. A Franklin stove has been inserted into the original fireplace. Directly in front of the fireplace, about eight feet from the center of the hearth, is a metal plate in the wooden floor. The metal plate wiggles and makes a slight noise when stepped on. The floors appear to be original, and

The inside hall at the Elias Hicks House. *Velsor Collection.*

the metal plate seems out of place. Access to the basement can be made from a door in the original kitchen or from the outside. The foundation of the home is all made of granite stones. As was the custom in homes built in 1740, there was a need for a root cellar. The root cellar was constructed underground on the east side of the house. It was dug from the existing floor of the cellar about seven feet under the ground. Originally, the cellar was dug out and supported after the hole was completed. In this case, the root cellar was large enough to hold the vegetables from the harvest for the duration of the winter without letting the vegetables freeze.

An important part of this story is the Quakers' testimonies against war. As pacifists, the Quakers refused to pay for anything connected to the Revolutionary War effort. Thus, in 1777, when orders were given by the Patriots who controlled Long Island to all residents to lend financial support to the war, the orders were not obeyed by members of the Society of Friends. Refusal to obey meant that members would be fined. In that same year, Patriots rode to the Seaman farm in Jericho and "took from Elias Hicks a pair of silver buckles worth eighteen shillings, two pair of stockings worth eighteen shillings and two handkerchiefs worth five shillings." Later that year, when Elias refused to pay for the construction of a military fortification, authorities took "a great coat worth one pound and six shillings." Elias was appointed by the Westbury Meeting to record the "Sufferings" of Friends due to the confiscation of goods. As the war progressed, many incidents were recorded, like when Patriots crossed the sound in their forty-foot whaleboats and attacked farmers sympathetic to the British, stealing money and goods and even torturing them to find hidden treasures. Elias recorded losses averaging two hundred pounds per year.[107]

As a result, as mentioned, many Quakers on Long Island began to build hidden closets to hide their valuables. Historians believe that the members of the Seaman/Hicks family in Jericho decided to close off the access to the root cellar at this time. It is believed that an access point was made from inside the house.[108] More granite was used to seal up the entrance to the root cellar from the basement. The base of the chimney was enlarged to accommodate a small stair from the first floor to the root cellar. The root cellar was then accessible through the floor of the dining room. This allowed the family to hide their valuables when they needed

The barn at the Elias Hicks House. *Velsor Collection.*

to. As the war progressed, many homes were raided for their food. On one recorded occasion when Elias was not at home, his wife, Jemima, was forced to give the Patriots wheat for payment. The wheat was stored in the barns.

After the war, members of the Society of Friends did not believe that they should pay taxes for the expense of the local ministers. Therefore, to keep their valuables safe from tax collectors, they hid their commodities in such secret spaces. When an opportunity arose to help an enslaved person to safety, the space was already available for the protection of the runaway person. In the years preceding the Civil War, the root cellar was used to hide such people. Many times, groups of enslaved people were brought to Jericho from New York. Valentine Hicks would make the arrangements through the members of other Quaker meetinghouses, and couriers were sent to find safe places for them to stay.[109]

# THE JACKSON HOUSE

In 1816, another young Quaker family moved to Jericho after inheriting a small house and farm. The little house was built in 1757 by Dr. James Townsend and his wife, Mary Hicks. In 1789, Dr. Townsend was elected to the U.S. Congress. Unfortunately, he died before he could accept the position. That same year, four of his seven children also passed away. Mary then sold the house and moved to live with the Townsend family in Oyster Bay. The house was purchased by John Jackson, a fourth-generation Jackson from the Robert Jackson line who was the brother of Thomas Jackson of Jerusalem. John married Charity Tredwell in 1765. They had four children. When she died, John married Margaret Townsend, and they had five children. Obadiah Jackson was John's third son, and he married Elizabeth Wright, who passed away. In 1804, Obadiah married Rachel Underhill Jackson.[110]

The couple moved to Jericho, and they had three children, who would have been about the same ages as Valentine Hicks's children, who lived across the street. William Jackson was born in 1813, and Elias Hicks was born in 1815. William inherited the farm, and when he married Sarah Tappan, it is believed that they built the larger part of the house that stands on top of the hill across the street from the Valentine Hicks House. They

The exterior of the Jackson/Malcolm Home. *Velsor Collection.*

had one child, Phebe Jackson, who later married James Malcolm. The house remained in the family until it was purchased by the County of Nassau in 2000. The Jackson family is believed to have maintained their family's interest in supporting the freedom efforts of enslaved people.

## JOHN AND REBECCA KETCHUM

In the early 1820s, John Ketchum brought his bride, Rebecca Sherman, to Jericho. Rebecca was born on September 9, 1792, in Jericho. She was the oldest child of Isaac and Margarett Fitzgerald Sherman. Several more children were born. Two died young, and then Margarett died. Isaac Sherman did not have a family member to help raise the children so they were "lent" to relatives. There is no record of where James grew up. Rebecca was raised by John Townsend and family in Oyster Bay, who were members of the Jericho Meeting. Rebecca lived in the Mill Pond

The Ketchum barn. *Velsor Collection.*

House just west of the village of Oyster Bay, near the millpond and the flour mill. When Rebecca married John Ketchum, she moved to the "Old Ketchum Place." The Ketchum farm was one mile east of the Jericho Meeting on the south side of Jericho Turnpike. Early photographs show that there was a large expanse of rolling farmland south of the main house. The house was not large, but it was placed among a series of large barns and nestled under a large black oak tree whose branches provided shade and protection for many years.[111]

John Ketchum and Rebecca "often took in runaways." These accounts were recorded in 1939 by Phebe Ketchum McAllister and informally published in "Family Affairs, or Go to Jericho." The book describes much of the everyday life of Jericho at the turn of the last century. Phebe wrote that she found out a great deal about her grandparents when she found a series of letters written to them from their children, William and Phebe, as well as from friends James and Lucretia Mott. The letters reveal that they were both very interested in the abolition of slavery and in women's suffrage, and she found many letters relating their parts in these controversies. Their home was a part of the "Underground Railway for the transmission of slaves to New England, though 25 miles from New York, driving a covered wagon, and return with Negroes who were afterward shipped across the Sound from Huntington or Cold Spring Harbor to Connecticut shore."[112]

John Ketchum wrote extensive letters to Isaac and Amy Post, who were originally from Westbury and Jericho and moved to Rochester, New York. Both were strong abolitionists, and John's letters discussed many of the political concerns of the Antislavery Society. His letters recorded many important issues concerning the feelings of the members of the local Society of Friends. Rebecca spent her time educating free and enslaved people, first in her home and later at the home of William and Sarah Tappan Jackson.

The Jackson Home is directly across Old Jericho Turnpike from the Jericho Meetinghouse. After it was purchased by the County of Nassau, the home retained the Malcolm name. When the home was used to hide and educate escaping slaves, it was owned by the Jackson family. I have confirmed that this home, the Jackson/Malcolm Home, played a very important part in the Underground Railroad on Long Island.

I received a thank-you call from the director of the Nassau County Historical Buildings in the spring of 2005. The conversation centered on the awarding of recognition for the Elias Hicks House and the Jericho Meetinghouse as part of the New York State Heritage Trail. During the conversation, I asked if I could have a tour of the Malcolm Home. The county needed funds for renovations and decided to allow a group to use the house as a designer showcase. I met the director at the house. He was very knowledgeable about the history of the house and the work of Dr. Malcolm, who was the husband of Phebe Jackson. He mentioned that the third floor was filled with artifacts and invited me to view it. We climbed an open staircase set against the interior wall ascending from the second floor to the third floor. At the top stair, there is a door. I was amazed at the amount of things that were still in the attic. The space runs the length of the newer addition, with large windows at either end. The beams are all exposed, framing the original wooden shingles that make up the roof.

Two items drew my attention. The first was the large number of school desks and old teaching supplies that were still there. The director asked me what I thought they were for. At the time, I did not make the whole connection, but Rebecca Ketchum was known to be a teacher for enslaved children in Jericho. Since this meeting, I have come across some information that Sarah Tappan Jackson kept a list of names of the families who attended the school. Rebecca and Sarah are believed to have hidden these names in the supporting beams to the third floor and another list behind the brick wall on the left-hand side of the original oven. The second item that raised

The supporting beams to the third floor of the Jackson/Malcolm Home. *Velsor Collection.*

my curiosity was the large wooden ladder that is permanently attached to the floor and mounted to a small opening in the roof. It was the custom in older homes to have a way to go to the roof to maintain the shingles. What I questioned was the obvious use the ladder has had over the years. Each rung of the ladder is worn as if it was continuously in use.

Between 1815 and 1865, the members of the Jericho community were assisting enslaved people to freedom. Evidence supports that families such as the Ketchums, Hickses, Jacksons and Willets, as well as the Willis home, took in enslaved people who were in need of shelter. When large groups of runaways came, they were divided up for their safety and to help the people blend in with the larger community. The Jackson/Malcolm Home is one of the largest homes in Jericho and is believed by historians to have employed kitchen and farmhands who were seeking freedom. Most importantly, the third floor of the house was used as a school. Not all of the members of the Jericho Meeting were aware of these arrangements, so it was important to keep the effort a secret.

There is evidence that on many occasions there was an increase in the black population as black helpers were integrated into the working community of

The ladder to the roof of the Jackson/Malcolm Home. *Velsor Collection.*

Jericho. One letter from Mary Jackson to Amy Post simply reads, "We have a young girl from the Brush helping with the whitening." Another letter from Mary Willis to Amy Post notes, "We have a young girl her name is Margaret staying with us for awhile she can read and is very polite." There are also

An exterior view of the Jackson/Malcolm Home. *Velsor Collection.*

references in the cooking diary from the Willets home (present-day Milleridge Inn), where the kitchen help mentions that there are extra women to help with the cooking. These were likely enslaved women who worked in Jericho until another shelter could be found to help them on their journey "up the trail" to another Hicksite Quaker community where they would be safe.[113]

In 1815, the Jackson/Malcolm Home was enlarged with the addition of a three-story house that is attached to the original home on the west side. The third floor of the new house provided ample space for living quarters for runaways, as well as a very large space for teaching children and adults. The original house built in 1757 by Dr. Townsend is also a three-story home, but the height of the floors gives it the appearance of a two-story house. The door to the ground floor is on the east side of the house and is hidden from the road. Access to the original house is on the second floor from the west side. As was the custom of the time, the kitchen was on the ground floor or in the basement of the home. There is a large fireplace along the north wall that was used for all of the household chores. The room is very dry and sunny. The addition that was designed tripled the size of the house. Connections were designed to unite the houses on the south side of the

A view from the roof of the Jackson/Malcolm Home. *Velsor Collection.*

original home. The ground floor of the original house is also the basement for the new house. It is an open space, with an entrance to the new house running through to a staircase in the eastern end of the basement. The staircase connects to the central hallway of the newer house. The first floors connect to the larger home through a small doorway on the western side of the house. There is a staircase in the original house that leads to a small loft room that connects to the larger house through a narrow opening cut between two supporting beams.[114]

Schooling for escaping slaves was necessary to protect the enslaved peoples' identities. Adults and children were given an opportunity to learn to read and write, as well as instruction in speech and social skills. Rebecca Ketchum and Sarah Jackson worked to help the runways act like Northern free blacks. Abigail Hicks helped to create papers to give them new identities. Groups of traveling runaways would stay for a number of months until arrangements could be made to move to the families north. A query would go out to another Hicksite meeting by courier, who would return with notification as to where to take the runaways. When it was dangerous, Valentine Hicks would arrange to move the enslaved families quickly at night to the Townsend family at the mill in Oyster Bay.[115]

*Above*: Mill Hill House. *Velsor Collection.*

*Left*: A hidden closet at the Mill Hill House. *Velsor Collection.*

The opening in the roof on the third floor faces north. The ladder was used to fix the shingles on the roof, and it also was used to make sure that runaways made it safely to the Mill Pond House in Oyster Bay. The north shore of Long Island has many hills as a result of the glacier deposits of the second ice age. The village of Jericho is located on one of the higher elevations on the north shore of Long Island. During the Revolutionary War, many of the trees were used for firewood, and farmers cleared the land to grow food. It is very possible that this opening in the roof was used as a way to ensure that runaways made their way safely to the George W. Townsend home on the millpond in Oyster Bay. In the dark of night, the light of a simple match could be seen from the opening of the Jackson house. In an effort to keep the movements of runaways a secret, groups often walked to Oyster Bay. A simple light could be followed from the opening in the roof of the Jackson Home. The group would follow present-day Route 106 north through East Norwich and down Mill River Road to the Mill Hill House. If it was not safe to continue the escape, or if the connections could not be made, the runaways were hidden in the basement of the house on Mill Hill Road.[116]

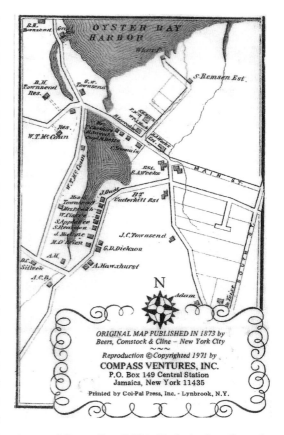

A map of Oyster Bay. *Published by Section Beers Comstock & Cline, 1873.*

The Townsends owned the property, and the structure was originally a sheep barn. George W. Townsend hid runaways there when it was not safe to travel. George was a member of the Jericho Meeting, but he felt that he should be paid for his work. When the members found out that he was being paid for his work, they encouraged him to leave the Society of Friends.[117] After this, his son, George C. Townsend, provided the transportation. In the 1840s, the barn was converted into a home. In the dining room, there is a china closet that unhooks and becomes a door to a hallway that connects to an outside door. The closet is large and was probably built to hide valuables and runaways. On a few occasions, the runaways were taken to Oak Neck (Bayville) to the old Seaman cabin to avoid the slave catchers.[118]

# OLD WESTBURY

The members of the Westbury Meeting were also helping enslaved people to freedom. The Hicks family gave land to establish Guinea Town, the first free black community in Old Westbury. The property was originally located on the corner of Glen Cove Road and the southwestern corner of the access road to the Long Island Expressway. The name Guinea, some historian have suggested, is connected to an ancestral home in Africa, while others attribute the name to the Guinea hens that were part of the wildlife on Long Island. In 1793, the members of the community established Guinea Town.[119] It became the home to many free blacks and served as a safe place for many runaways, who could hide in plain view of other formerly enslaved people. Unlike the Brush, where people could make a living at the mill or by farming the waters of the inlets of the south shore, Guinea Town was located at the edge of the Hempstead Plains, where farming was the major industry. By 1830, the community had its own church and school that was built by the Charity Society. The early maps show a number of homes in proximity of the church. The residents of Guinea Town worked on the Quaker farms located in Old Westbury and present-day Wheatly.

Valentine Hicks of Jericho and his brother Isaac of Old Westbury maintained their membership with the Westbury Friends Meeting. Their father, Samuel Hicks, married Phebe Seaman.[120] They had five children: Isaac, Elizabeth, Samuel, Valentine and Phebe. Samuel Hicks's father died when he was very young. He was brought up as a member of the Westbury Meeting, learned how to be a tailor and became quite prosperous.[121] Isaac,

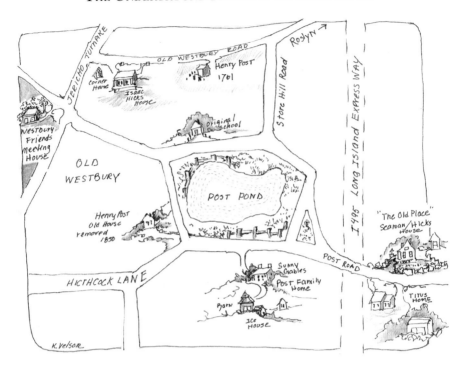

A map of Old Westbury. *Velsor Collection.*

Westbury Friends Meeting. *Velsor Collection.*

his eldest son, was also trained as a tailor, and he supplemented his work by teaching at the Westbury School. He earned a stipend of twelve dollars per month. Isaac asked for a raise, but the school board members denied his request. With his savings and a loan from his father, Isaac left Westbury for New York City. In 1789, Isaac Hicks purchased a grocery store on Water Street. He presented the New York Meeting with a certificate from the Westbury Meeting. With the support of local Quakers, the business prospered. The year 1790 was one of great change in Isaac Hicks's life because he married Sarah Doughty, moved into a house on Everitt Street in Brooklyn and sold the grocery store. He then became a junior partner in a whale oil trading firm with a man named John Alsop, who was from Nantucket, Massachusetts. As the business grew, Hicks chartered boats and then organized a charter company to conduct international trade—particularly with France, Ireland and Russia—in American-made products.[122]

Isaac Hicks was one of the original members of the Manumission Society in New York City. This was an organization that worked in many ways to help enslaved people reach safety. The members supplied money to assist escaping slaves and campaigned against slavery in New York State. Isaac Hicks actively pursued slave catchers. The New York Historical Library transferred the minutes from the Manumission Society onto microfilm. Reading through the records in 1801, I found an entry for February:

*Isaac Hicks presented a bill for expenses amount* [of] *$49.70* [incurred] *in pursuing a vessel wh*[ich], *it was succumbed it was a boat carrying several Blacks for which the chairman is requested to give a warrant on the treasurer.*[123]

Isaac Hicks stopped the ship off Staten Island and recaptured the kidnapped blacks. Kidnapping—or "blackbirding," as it was sometimes referred to—was common in New York City. The minutes of a June 27 meeting of the same year provided a record of Hicks having witnessed the recapture of free blacks who were from Flatbush.[124] The family was on the boat docked in Brooklyn when Isaac heard the sounds of people inside. He asked who was on board. He found a freed black family who were being kidnapped for the purpose of selling the family into slavery in the South.

Isaac Hicks retired from the shipping business in 1802 and commissioned Thomas Buckley and Andrew Cook to build a house for his family in what is now called Old Westbury.[125] Both a relative and a close friend of Elias Hicks, Isaac Hicks continued with his antislavery activities. He traveled with

Elias as he spread his ministry and used the Quaker connections he had established in his shipping business to raise funds for the African Free School in New York City.

Isaac and Sara Doughty Hicks had six children: John D., Robert, Benjamin, Isaac, Elizabeth and Mary. Isaac Hicks Sr. died suddenly in 1820. Sarah never remarried, but she lived in the home that is still on Old Westbury Road in Old Westbury. Their eldest son, John, was born in 1791 and married Sarah Rushmore. They lived in the old house, now on the Phipps estate. They had seven children: Lydia, Isaac, Stephen, Valentine, Samuel, John S. and Walter.

In 1824, John Hicks was able to travel with his uncle Elias for eight months. When he was traveling, he wrote to Sarah about the welfare of the farm: "I feel no uneasiness about the welfare of the farm as I thyself fully competent to it. I suppose the barn is done, you are getting in the corn, carting wood and soon be ready for winter grain, 1824." In another letter, dated 1825, he wrote, "I think I can feel easy to build a new house another year if nothing hinders and try to enjoy our blessings in moderation so that they may be lasting and hoard up wealth for spoiling our dear off spring I am glad we never gave way to extravagance as so many I have seen among friends. May we keep free from it is my desire."

During this time, John's mother, Sara Hicks, took a fugitive into her home. His name was Elikiam Levi. He lived on her farm and managed the farm's affairs. John's son Isaac, when he was twenty years old, helped Elikiam Levi to establish the New Light Baptist Church in Grantville.[126] This property was originally part of the Richard Powell farm of Westbury. Elikiam Levi and his descendants—Carman, Willis, Charles Levi (Willis's son) and others—all owned homes in Grantville. Charles Levi had a herd of twenty-five cows that wandered the open fields known as the Hempstead Plains. Established in 1642, the early settlers used the plains for grazing the animals and the Meadow Brook River for water. He also had a business of selling carloads of brewer's grains for feed to the local farmers, as well as shipping pickles and other farm crops into New York City. Elikiam remained a minister and had three more congregations, with one in Lakeville (the church still stands on Lakeville Road). He also traveled to the Quaker communities of Jerusalem and Jericho.[127]

This neighborhood has increased in size. The original Grantville was in Westbury on the west end of the community. The parcel of land extended north from Union Avenue or Brush Hollow Road, east to Grand Avenue, south to Railroad Avenue and west to School Street. Originally, this neighborhood was farmland, like most of Long Island. Ester Emory, noted local historian, wrote about John Wheeler, whom her father knew was "a real runaway." Her father told the story of how he escaped from the South with the help of Hicksite Quakers and came to Westbury to live. First, he constructed a small home in the cedar swamp and made shingles. Then he worked for the Westbury Friends Meetinghouse and eventually bought his own home in Grantville. Henry Hicks told the story of Charles Mitchell, who was a runaway. Charles owned a farm where Scally Place is located and mentioned Edwin Hughes, who lived in Grantville with his wife.[128]

# THE OLD PLACE

Having a fugitive slave live in Grandmother Sara Hicks's home must have influenced Lydia and Benjamin to carry on the family's antislavery sentiments. Lydia Hicks married her cousin, Joseph Hicks. They lived in the Old Place in Old Westbury. This house was originally the Old Seaman Hicks House. Their oldest son, Benjamin, ran the Roslyn Mill. Benjamin had a sister, Rachael Hicks, who became an artist and photographer. Rachael Hicks told stories about runaways coming to the farm by wagon and being taken to Long Island Sound for passage to Westchester County.[129]

I was sitting in my office on a very chilly November afternoon when the phone rang. I hesitated and picked up the phone. After introducing myself, I heard a very low voice on the other end asking me if I "was the lady." "Excuse me?" I responded. "Are you the lady who is researching the Underground Railroad?" "Yes." I waited for her response. "I am a medium…and I am renting this house, the Old Place…You need to save the house." I was a little confused. What is a medium? I had to think back and try to put the information together. I agreed to meet her the next day at about 4:00 p.m. at the Old Place.

The Old Place is on Post Road just north of the Long Island Expressway. The house is tucked behind a long red brick wall on the west side of the road. There is a large black wrought-iron gate with a grand entrance. As I drove onto the property, the Old Place was on the left-hand side. I climbed out of my car and looked at the front of the house, and I was confronted with three front doors. There is one in the center of the house, one to the left and one on the right. The door on the

The Old Place. *Rachael Hicks, Nassau County Historical Collection.*

The original house at the Old Place. *Rachael Hicks, Nassau County Historical Collection.*

left opened, and for the first time in my life, I engaged in a conversation with a medium.

She gladly escorted me through the home. It was lovely, with a tiny kitchen in the front of the house, a grand room with a fireplace and many windows facing south. There was a central hall and another front door with a large porch. We climbed an old staircase up to the second floor and found many bedrooms that seemed to be connected somehow. As we walked through the second floor, she talked about her work and asked if I could see the Quaker women in the house. She was surprised that I did not see them. We went outside and walked around the foundation. The house is really a twin house. There are two houses built side by side, and they share a wall. The oldest part of the house is on the east side. The medium explained to me that a client had come for a reading, and as she was preparing to make a connection, all of a sudden the room filled with Quaker women dressed in bonnets and aprons. After the reading, she asked her client what she had learned. Her client said that her Quaker relatives were afraid that the house was going to be torn down and that she needed to "find the lady" who could save the Old Place. Working with the Society for Long Island Antiquities, we joined with the Village of Old Westbury and saved the house from the hands of the developer.

I have since returned to the house, and I have found evidence of hiding places in the newer part of the house. The original Seaman home was built in 1695. The front door of the newer section of the house faces north. There is a central hall with a stair to the second floor. At the top of the stair is a closet, and in the back of the closet is a second door that opens to a space between the two houses. This space may have been created to hide valuables from the tax collectors. On the bottom floor to the right of the staircase is a long hallway to the kitchen. On the south wall of the kitchen is a staircase to the attic. Here Rachael Hicks confirmed that enslaved people were kept for safety.

Rachael Hicks was born at the Old Place in 1857. As a child living in the house, she remembered what her older brother and sister later told her. This is her story:

> The older children were carefully instructed not to discuss any unusual movements in the house; they were forbidden to inform their schoolmates of anything curious that they apprehended. The children remember watching their mother Lydia preparing large amounts of food and placing it in the day hampers. The next day the food would be gone. They also remember

The Old Place today. *Velsor Collection.*

The shearing of the sheep. *Rachael Hicks, Nassau County Historical Collection.*

*hearing mysterious noises in the night while they were sleeping. They would
hear the wagon wheels approaching the kitchen door then the noise of the
water being "squeezed and water splashed." Although there were no signs
of the visitors the next day, when night fell again, the group of fugitives
would quietly descend the stairs to the kitchen; and the wagon wheels would
be heard once more as they moved away toward Long Island Sound.*

It was not until after the Civil War that Rachel was told the secret of
the Old Place They also learned how the fugitives would stop here while a
connection was made to other Hicksite Quaker friends across Long Island
Sound, through Connecticut and upper New England to Canada.[130]
There are some funny tales that have been kept in the Hicks family
papers about the Old Place. One tells of how the Hicks family dressed up
a young man in Grandma's clothes and took him to the water. Another
said that an enslaved person was hidden in a "hogshead" and taken to
Long Island Sound.[131]

# THE JOHN POST FAMILY FROM LONG ISLAND

Another very prominent Quaker family who were members of the Westbury
Meeting were the Post family. This branch of the family is descended from
John Post of South Hampton, New York. His son, Richard Post II, was
born in 1684. Richard and his wife, Jeremiah, were Quakers who moved
to Westbury to settle among the Hicks and Willis families on present-day
Old Westbury Road and Post Road in Westbury. Richard II and Jeremiah
Post had four children: Richard III, Joseph, John and a daughter, Phebe.
Richard III's oldest son, Henry, was born in 1733 and married Mary Titus
in 1761. They had a son, Edmund, who was born in 1762. Edmund married
Catherine Willets in 1788. They had four children: Phebe (1790–1845),
Edmund (1792–1832), Isaac (1798–1872) and Joseph (1803–1888). The two
youngest brothers, Joseph and Isaac, were very close. Phebe Post married
Henry Willis. All four of them became active in the antislavery efforts. The
family home became the home of Joseph and Mary Robbins Post, and it is
located directly south of the Old Place on Post Road.[132]
I received a number of grants to travel to the University of Rochester
to read the correspondence between Joseph Post and Mary Robbins Post

and between other Quakers from Long Island and Isaac and Amy Post. Much of the information here has come from these letters. They are all handwritten and often difficult to read. If the letter contained information about escaping slaves, it was often hidden within a sentence or written like a child writing in an autograph book. I saw letters written in circles or written like a checkerboard, with sentences going one way and then another. The most difficult letters to read were the ones in which a space was left between each line one direction, and then the letter was turned upside down and a line was written in the other direction. It was well worth the read. What I found was enough information to investigate the stories compiled in this volume.

# Isaac and Amy Post

Isaac Post married Hannah Kirby from the Jericho Meeting on Long Island and moved upstate to Scipio in central New York. Hannah died in 1827 soon after having their second child. Her sister, Amy Kirby, went to Scipio and cared for the children, Mary and Henry. In 1829, Isaac and Amy were married and moved to Rochester, New York. They had two children, Joseph and Jacob, born in 1830 and 1834, respectively. Isaac and Amy Post were very outspoken against slavery and helped to form a network of Friends who assisted runaways. Their home became a center for traveling antislavery people such as William Lloyd Garrison, Lucretia Mott, Harriet Jacobs, Sojourner Truth, Susan B. Anthony and Frederick Douglass. Isaac and Amy Post helped Douglass assist runaways fleeing to Canada. Together, they produced the *North Star* newspaper. Joseph Post, Isaac's brother, actively sought subscriptions from people on Long Island.[133]

In 1828, Joseph married Mary Robbins Post from Jericho. Mary was a Quaker and the daughter of Willet and Esther Seaman Robbins of Jericho. Joseph and Mary lived in Old Westbury on a farm by the Westbury Pond. The pond today is surrounded by Post Road and remains a landmark to all who have traveled this road. The house was built before the American Revolution and was occupied by generations of Post family members until the expansion of the Long Island Expressway in 1960. When the house was sold, family members came to organize the myriad family artifacts that had accumulated over the century of ownership. In the attic of the

A view of Post Pond. *Velsor Collection.*

The Post family home. *Velsor Collection.*

house, the family found copies of antislavery newspapers such as the *Liberator* (written by William Lloyd Garrison), the *North Star* and even the *Pennsylvania Freeman*. Also found was the suitcase that Joseph Post took to the Nine Partners School.[134]

# JOSEPH AND MARY ROBBINS POST

Joseph was known to be fearless in his work against slavery. He could always be counted on to divert slave catchers and to be quick to respond to potential dangers. He and Mary provided shelter to individuals and to families who needed a safe place to stay. Some letters make a reference to a family legend that the icehouse on the farm was also used to house escaping slaves. Another story tells that Joseph was "shameless" in his ability to quickly respond to slave catchers, who asked, "Who are these Black children staying on your farm?" Joseph simply responded that "they were all his children." To Joseph's delight, the slave catcher climbed into his wagon and left them alone. His outspoken words and actions earned him a great deal of respect among the Quakers on Long Island. They were good friends with antislavery relatives like Lucretia Mott and Aaron Macy Powell. They held antislavery meetings in their home on Post Road. The Quaker meetinghouses were not approved to have antislavery meetings, so in an attempt to facilitate the effort, Joseph and Mary opened their home to meetings. They would simply place chairs in the living room, with planks of wood connecting one chair to the next, to accommodate the large crowds of people from Jericho and Westbury Meetings.[135]

In a letter written in 1848 from Mary R. Post to Isaac and Amy Post, Mary related a portion of a story, leaving it up to the reader to interpret a series of events that transpired near their home: "Have had some friends today. After they left we had the papers which Joseph has been reading very diligently until a few minutes ago when he was sent for over to our tenant ____. [Aaron Bunn] had dislocated his jaw and is in much distress, they have gone for the Dr. [Selah Carll]."

Aaron Bunn was a runaway slave who came to Old Westbury and later was a "tenant" who lived on a farm near the Post home. Bunn was a fugitive from Virginia and had escaped and joined a group of fugitives that was moving north through the Hicksite Quaker network. He decided to stay

The icehouse at the Post family home. *Velsor Collection.*

in Westbury rather than move north with the group. Bunn often escorted groups of people to safety. He felt that he was doing God's work and was never afraid for his life. On one particular night, Bunn was taking a group from the Post home (note Mary's reference to "friends") across a field on the Titus farm. The trespassers were in a cornfield just west of the Post home when they were caught. Seeing the group crossing his property, Mr. Titus shot his gun off in the air. Bunn quickly ran to take the gun from Mr. Titus, and Mr. Titus punched him in the face. Bunn never fired the gun. He simply handed it back to Mr. Titus, saying, "Now why did you go and do that for?" Mary did not mention the potential danger, but she continued to stay awake until it was resolved, even though it was late:[136]

> *On Joseph's leaving I resolve to take up my pen late as it is…Have just read Fredric's letter to master Auld. It is not grand. I hope he will profit by such faithful expostulations and such evident signs of progress in his once slave and be induced to act honestly…By the by Samuel Smith has been down among the slaves and slaveholders and he feels (so we hear) less objection to slavery than before, they were so happy and he thought them*

A view of Old Westbury farmland. *Rachael Hicks, Nassau County Historical Collection.*

*better off than the free ones around here. Alass, alass for anyone who can come to such a conclusion, they must very nearly approach that state even more to be dreaded-hardness of heart. It really seems dreadful to hear such sentiments advanced.*

By 1850, with the onset of the Fugitive Slave Law Mary Robbins Post told a story to Isaac, her brother-in-law, in the middle of a discussion about everyday life, in a letter dated April 18?2. Mary wrote, "[S]uppose you know of this poor slave man is sure off from New York how terrible to think of the misery and despair this diabolical law has inflicted." The implication of this powerful statement is that the "poor slave man" was living in New York City. When the slave catcher came to the city, the self-emancipated man, being a fugitive, needed to find a place to go. He sought the help of a Quaker, who sent him to the Post family on Long Island for safety. Later in the letter, she mentioned that the neighbor was shooting his rifle in the air because a runaway was trying to hide in his barn. In another letter, dated April 27, 185?, the "poor slave man sent out from New York—[with a] small attached piece of paper." It is not a far reach to think that the second letter, written a week later, could have been to notify Isaac that the runaway slave was on his way to Rochester.

Each group of runaways needed to cross over Long Island Sound. Some historians believe that Benjamin Hicks, the father of Rachael Hicks, assisted with the escapes when he owned and operated the Roslyn Mill. The road from the Post family home and the Old Place to the mill is a short and private route through Quaker farms. Today, the route would be west from Post Road on the access road of the Long Island Expressway running from

The Roslyn Mill. *Velsor Collection.*

Red Ground Road north to Roslyn Pond to the back of the Roslyn Mill. A boat would have been waiting during a high tide, when the group in the dark of night could quietly sail across the sound. Benjamin was also related to another family who assisted runaways: the Mott family from Cowneck, Sands Point and in Mamaroneck in Westchester County, New York.[137]

## ROBERT AND MARY UNDERHILL MOTT HICKS

Benjamin Hicks's uncle was Robert Hicks, the second son of Isaac Hicks. Robert Hicks married Mary Underhill Mott at Premium Point in 1814. Before his marriage, he attended the Nine Partners School and then returned to Westbury in 1813. Robert was greatly influenced by Elias Hicks. While living in Westbury, he occupied the corner house on his father's property. Robert Hicks was fearless in his efforts to assist runaway slaves. From this house, Robert offered shelter to runaways by giving them a good meal and providing a safe route.

The corner house. *Velsor Collection.*

He began his efforts first in Westbury and later operated out of his own home in New York City. Like his father, he was a steadfast Hicksite Quaker, zealous in his testimonies. An active member of the New York Manumission Society, he was brazen with his actions and very outspoken during meetings. To this extent, he helped to plan escapes and routes for runaways. From New York City, he would bring runways to the Old Mott Homestead in Cowneck. When another safe home could be found, the runaways would be sent across the sound to Premium Point, to Mamaroneck and to New Rochelle, where the group would be met by a family member who would then take the runaways to the next stop on their journey to freedom.[138]

Some humorous stories have been remembered about Robert's heroic deeds. One such story, told and retold in Hicks family circles, has Robert Hicks dressing an escaping slave in his wife's clothes, complete with a veil on her head. His brother-in-law, Richard Mott, then led the escaping slave past her owner's store and escorted her to a sloop owned by his relative, Samuel Mott, who then took the woman to Long Island and to safety.[139]

The connections to Westchester County, New York, came from an original letter written by Wilmer in 1939. Mary Underhill Mott Hicks was related to Joseph Carpenter of New Rochelle through her mother's family. Carpenter, a member of the New Rochelle Friends Meeting, actively loved and supported the African population of New Rochelle. He routinely opened his home to orphans and worked to free slaves through his work with the Underground Railroad. Remembered as a gentle and lovable man with a large circle of friends, Carpenter became a kind of folk hero. Friends constantly made requests for photographs of him with the orphans for whom he cared. He provided the first stop on the Underground Railroad going north from New York City.[140] His home was close to the Mott home at Premium Point, which made it an ideal stop for slaves escaping through Long Island or from New York City. Carpenter provided the first in a trail of safe places scattered throughout Westchester County and upstate New York. Under cover of night, runaways and conductors moved from his home to that of Joseph Pierce, located in Pleasantville, New York. The home of Judge Jay, Pierce's brother-in-law, provided the third stop on the route. Runaways next went to the home of David Irish in Quaker Hill, near the Oblong Quaker Meetinghouse.[141]

# THE STORY OF LEVI TRUSTY

E qually as important as the stories of enslaved people moving north from Long Island are the stories of those who traveled from the South and found safety with the Hicksite Quakers on Long Island. One of the first stories that I came across about the Underground Railroad on Long Island was about Henry Highland Garnet. The story is told by Dr. James McCune Smith as an introduction to the "Memorial Discourse" by Reverend Henry Highland Garnet, delivered in the hall of the House of Representatives in Washington City, D.C., on the Sabbath, February 12, 1865.

As a young man, Henry came back from a sailing mission from Cuba and was furious when he found that his parents' home had been ransacked by a slave catcher. Outraged, Henry bought a clasp knife and walked up and down the streets of Manhattan, swinging it back and forth and threatening the life of the attacker. He was soon silenced by members of the Society of Friends and brought to the home of Thomas Willis in Jericho, New York.

I was so intrigued by the story that I wrote a grant to investigate the route that he and his family took in 1824, from Maryland to New York City. I was very excited when the grant was approved. I immediately looked for the location of his family home as stated in the discourse: New Market Square in Kent County, Maryland. Kent County is on the eastern shore of the Chesapeake about two hours south of Philadelphia. I was looking forward to traveling down the Chesapeake until I discovered that New Market Square, Maryland,[142] is in the western part of the state next to Frederick, Maryland. Once again, I found myself asking a question and finding my way down a different path than other researchers had traveled. Rather than looking for a reference to a town named New Market in Kent County, I acted on my own instincts. It is very possible that a nine-year-old boy escaping from slavery in 1824 would not have known what county in Maryland he came from. It takes about eight hours to travel by car from Long Island to Frederick, Maryland. This is the story that I found.

Levi Trusty was born in New Market Square, Maryland, in 1815. His boyhood home is northeast of Frederick, Maryland. Levi's paternal grandfather, Joseph, worked for Colonel Spencer. Joseph was a tall man who was admired for his "unbending integrity" and strength of character. These qualities led to the decision to give him status like a freeman from his Quaker master, Colonel Spencer.[143] Joseph was trained as a shoemaker, a skill that few blacks were taught. Shoes were seen as a vehicle for escaping. Perhaps this is why his last name was Trusty—he was trusted by members of his community. He had a son, Joseph, who married Henrietta, who is remembered for being very industrious and pious. Joseph and Henrietta had a son, Levi, who grew up to be tall like his grandfather.

Levi grew so fast that by the age of ten he was big enough to "do the work of a man." He was so big for his age that as a young child Levi remembered that the white ladies in Maryland were afraid of him. He knew that the ladies were afraid of him by the "look in their eyes when they met him." The published record of the escape and life of Levi Trusty was written in a brief memoir by James McCune Smith in 1866. He wrote that Colonel Spencer died in 1824, and in his will, he gave all of his possessions to his brother, Isaac, and sundry nephews.[144] "These heirs took a different view from their testator [man with a valid will] of the Patriarchal Institution. They determined to exercise the Constitutional rights to the fullest extent and reduce those who had hither to borne the names of slaves down, to bear the yoke of degradation of slavery."[145]

I was confused by this statement. Did the beneficiaries of the estate inherit slaves? The Frederick Historical Society was an excellent source of information. The librarian suggested that I read *The Quaker Records of Northern Maryland*. These records show that Colonel Spencer gave his possessions to his grandson William in 1814. William and his wife, Ury (Marks) Spencer, were both Quakers and lived in New Market Square. I also checked the census records for the state of Maryland, and they indicated that they had two slaves over forty-five and seven other people who (were not Indians) living with them. Could this have been the Trusty family?

The first settlers in Frederick County, Maryland, were searching for good farmland and a favorable climate in proximity to markets to sell their produce. In 1743, a land grant was given by Lord Baltimore to John Dorsey Jr. This was one of the first tracts of land in New Market. The farmers of New Market were so successful that by 1790, Frederick County was the largest wheat producing county in all of the thirteen states and one of the most productive agricultural counties in Maryland. The county's population at the time was 30,791 people.[146]

Moving produce and livestock to market became difficult because there were only foot trails. Many farmers needed shelter on the road. As a result, small villages and towns emerged along the road to Baltimore. One such town was New Market Square, located eight miles east of Frederick at a crossroads that was originally two Indian trails. One trail led to the mineral mines in southern Maryland, and the other was known as the Great Indian Trail, which led west. Today, this crossroads is U.S. 40 and Interstate 70.[147]

The first settlers to New Market were Quakers from the Philadelphia Meeting. They were the founders of the Bush Creek Meetinghouse in Monrovia, Maryland, three miles east of New Market. New Market Square

The slave market, New Market, Maryland. *Velsor Collection.*

is a planned community with one main road running through town and two side streets running parallel to the main street, with connecting alleyways linking homes that were built on small lots. Today, the community is referred to as New Market. In 1814, William and Ury Spencer moved to New Market and attended the Bush Creek Meeting.[148]

Maryland was a border state concerning the issue of slavery. Most slave owners, including Quakers, maintained that as long as they fed and provided shelter for enslaved people, it was acceptable. A change in attitude began to take hold in 1749. Elias Hicks traveled extensively, spreading the word against slavery. In reviewing the Post family letters compiled by Margery Post Abbott, I found this note from Isaac Hicks to his wife, Sarah. The letter is dated 1813:

*That we have attended Deer Creek, Little Falls & Gunpowder Meetings since we crossed the Susquehannah & yesterday attended on Monthly Meeting in this city & today intend to be at the others…We have been kindly treated & well received wherever we have been & particularly so in this city, although Uncle [Elias Hicks] has been very close on the subject of meddling with politick war & produce, slavery, tobacco etc.…leaving this city after meeting today & proceed to Elk Ridge & to Sandy Spring, Indian Spring & Alexandria & Washington four whence.*

The work of Elias Hicks and Isaac changed the minds of many Quakers in Maryland on the issues surrounding slavery. The final disentanglement of the question among Quakers appeared during the Hicksite and Orthodox separation in 1828. Friends who followed the teachings of Elias Hicks (Hicksites) believed that immediate action was needed to free enslaved people from bondage, while non-Hicksites, called Orthodox Quakers, believed in a gradual emancipation. The members of the Philadelphia Yearly Meeting, including the members of the Bush Creek Meeting and Sandy Spring Meeting, were Hicksite Quakers.[149]

Slavery existed in Frederick County in the early 1820s. New Market had an active market for the sale of enslaved people. These were recorded in many ads in the *Frederick Town Herald* in 1824. William Spencer was a member of the Bush Creek Meeting and was therefore a Hicksite Quaker. It is realistic to assume that the seven people working for William Spencer were held by a contract to work for the Spencer family because it was not safe for them to be freed in a slaveholding state.[150]

A complete review of all property records in Frederick County revealed that William Spencer did not own property (slaves) or land in Frederick. The

A Negro Man for Sale,

About 22 years of age, and wh —— is a good shoemaker.

*Enquire of the Printer.*

May 29

FOR SALE,

A negro Girl about 18 years old

Who has been accustomed to house wor! She will be sold on liberal terms. For fu: ther particulars enquire of the subscribe at the post office in Liberty.

JAMES REED.

May 29

Military Notice.

The young men of the neighborhood New Market and Liberty, who are desirou of forming a TROOP of HORSE, are re: pectfully invited to meet at Mr. Thoma Jones' tavern, in Liberty, at 2 o'clock P. on Saturday 5th of June next.

*Fredrick Town Herald*, May 8, 1824. *Fredrick Public Library, Historical Collection.*

census does show two slaves over forty-five and seven other people except Indians (not taxed). The *Frederick Town Herald* during this time had many listings for property to rent. William Spencer may have rented, or he may have lived on the property owned by his in-laws' family.[151]

James McCune Smith wrote that Colonel Spencer, who was a bachelor, died in 1824, and his relatives decided to sell his former slaves. The census records, however, show that Colonel Spencer died in 1814. A complete review of the property records of Frederick County, Maryland, shows that there was an indenture held by Martha Spencer for four enslaved people. Samuel Howard was due to pay the last installment in May 1824. Levi was born in 1815 after Colonel Spencer died.[152] For whatever reason, the family decided that it would be best to leave Maryland and go north to a free state. I was able to find some ads for the sale of enslaved people that matched the story, but no real connection could be made.

James McCune Smith also wrote about the Trusty family's decision to leave New Market:

*As they made no secret of their intentions, it reached the ears of the Trusty' a portion of who headed by [Levi's] father held a family council, where in they opened a new volume, in which, forgetful of "contract" and constitutional obligations, they made sundry entries treating their own rights to their Liberty! Within a few weeks after the death of Col. Spence, a family exodus was planned and carried out in the following manner. Permission having been obtained to attend the funeral of a relative at some few miles distances, eleven in number started in the same night on that sad errand ostensibly, but really with hearts which the North Star lit up with its wondrous joys, to the liberty seeking slaves. A covered wagon awaited them in a piece of woods; they got in and kept on till near daybreak, when they left the wagon and concealed themselves in the woods until night. Henry's mother, sister and seven others, including himself, composed this company. They have not, to this day, returned from the funeral, although all of them, except the subject of this memoir, having bountifully partaken of the blessings of liberty, are gone on a longer and higher pilgrimage.*[153]

It is reasonable to believe that the family was approached by a Quaker missionary who traveled to the Bush Creek Meeting. The decision to escape was prompted by this messenger, who told the family to go to the Sandy Spring Meetinghouse, where they would then be helped to reach freedom. A group of eleven people would have been hard to conceal. This is why they took the wagon to a funeral, saying that they would return. As the group reached each meetinghouse, another messenger or scout would direct them to another stop. Following the path from one Hicksite meeting to the next, they would have gone north to Elk Ridge, then to the Little Falls Meeting or to Gun Powder Falls and finally north to Deer Creek Meeting. The Deer Creek Meeting in Darlington, Maryland, is located on the south bank of the Susquehanna River.[154] Members would have told the family to travel north on present-day Route 1 to the home of Thomas Garret in Wilmington, Delaware.[155]

*For several days they slept in the woods and swamps, traveling all night long. Henry [Levi], now nine years old, kept up with the fugitives until his little limbs gave out, when his father and uncles took turns in carrying him upon their backs. After weary travel by night and partial rest by day, they left*

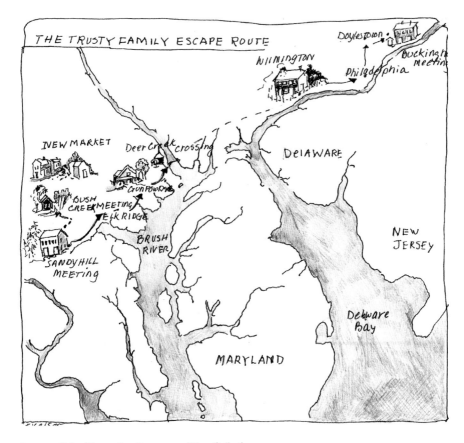

A map of the Trusty family escape. *Velsor Collection.*

*for Willington, Del. And that ever to remember half-way house for pilgrims
on the road to Freedom, the barn of Thomas Garret, the good Quaker, the
noble-hearted philanthropist, to whom so many thousands of our brethren,
on the way to Liberty, are indebted for shelter and sustenance.*[156]

Thomas Garret established a business in the Quaker Hill section of
Wilmington. The Trusty family would have been brought by a messenger to
the barn to stay. Here the group of eleven was divided for safety. Levi Trusty
and his family went northward up the Delaware River, and his uncle and his
family went across the river to New Jersey.

I wanted to find the actual path taken by the Trusty family from
Wilmington to New Hope, Pennsylvania. I first visited the New Hope
Historical Society, and there was nothing in its records that helped me
to make any connections. I then traveled to the Bucks County Historical

Society, located in a Doylestown, Pennsylvania. I was overwhelmed by the size of the Mercer Museum, formerly known as the Fonthill Castle. The collection features many preindustrial tools and early American artifacts, as well as an extensive display of Mennonite tiles. I found my way to the historical collection and decided to just find a seat at one of the long library desks. I was disoriented and needed to gather my thoughts. As I waited, I noticed a book that had been left on the desk: *An Illustrated History of Bucks County*. I was glancing through the pictures when I found a photograph of the Buckingham Meeting. A small caption read, "Buckingham Friends School 1794. Centerville [Lahaska] Pennsylvania." I laughed. I had just traveled through Lahaska on my way from New Hope to Dolyestown, Pennsylvania. Was this where the Trusty family lived? I found the reference to the school.

The school began with a recommendation from the Philadelphia Yearly Meeting in 1793. In May 1794, the Buckingham Meeting authorized the subscription fund. "[S]hould as well go towards the education of the bound apprentices of the members of this meeting though they may not be membership." Within two years, the Monthly Meeting was on record as having a concern for educating free blacks. Was this where Levi attended school? Further research confirmed that the Buckingham Meeting was Hicksite. In 1790, there were 173 dwellings in Centerville, with 188 outbuildings. This was a large Quaker farming community, with 1,137 white people and 73 black people. As I was jotting notes into my book, I glanced up and noticed that a woman had taken a seat across the table from me. I smiled. She asked me what I was reading. I told her briefly what I was researching. I do not know what the chances are of sitting across from a person who has similar interests.

She explained to me that across the street from the Buckingham Meeting there is a road that runs through the farmland and then climbs up a high hill. On top of the hill is the site of the first black community in Centerville, on Mount Gilead. There is a small church and a cemetery that tells the story of the escaping families who came to Centerville for safety. We talked about the work of Charles Blockson, noted scholar of the Underground Railroad and lifelong resident of Norristown, Pennsylvania. He has researched the trails running north of Philadelphia using Old York Road. His work suggests that connections were made through the meetinghouses from Jenkintown to Willow Grove, Horsham, Warminister and Doylestown. In Doylestown, the route that separated the Trusty family would have taken Old York Road to Centerville; today, this village is called Lahaska, Pennsylvania.[157]

The excitement of finding the community known as Mount Gilead was exhilarating. It was a warm summer's day. I had left Long Island at about 7:00 a.m. and arrived in New Hope by 10:00 a.m. After a short stay, I was in Doylestown by 1:00 p.m., and by 2:30 p.m., I had found the information to help me put the story together. As I drove back down Old York Road, I reflected on the many stone farmhouses with white fences and tall shady trees. I found the meetinghouse on the left and drove into the parking lot. The stone school is set off the road and today is a well-established private Friends school. The meetinghouse is large, and the cemetery seems to go on for acres.

My instructions were to turn at the first road across from the meetinghouse. As I drove down the road away from Old York Road, I could sense more of the feeling for the countryside. This must have been where the Trusty family had lived among the Quaker families at the foot of the hill. The road began to climb, and I was amazed at the small white AME church and cemetery. There was a handwritten sign on a large piece of plywood attached to the front of the church:

Buckingham Friends Meetinghouse. *Velsor Collection.*

Mount Gilead. *Velsor Collection.*

## MT. GILEAD A.M.E. CHURCH

*Pioneers at the turn of the century would make their way up the hill at night carrying lanterns to the regular "camp meetings." Before the Civil War Bucks County was a hideout for slaves in Little Mt. Gilead caves and in the cellars of old farmhouses.*[158]

The Trusty family traveled with the assistance of Quakers from the Philadelphia Meeting, and they were escorted to Centerville. Several members of the Buckingham Meeting agreed to take the travelers in. The journey took a fortnight, two weeks in total. The family lived here from 1824 to 1826. The family was divided among a number of families to protect their identities, just as Jericho runaways could hide in plain view among different families. The census shows that there was a small population of blacks; therefore, a large number of runaways in one family would be questioned. At the age of nine, Levi had never heard about school. All he knew was that he was big enough to "do a man's job." The family who took him in gave him nice clothes to wear and a pillow to rest his head on. Levi was very

Buckingham Friends School. *Velsor Collection.*

grateful for the pillow and the safe place to sleep. He worked in the laundry of the home. He helped with the towels and sheets and remembered that the shoes he was given were too big for him so he had to shuffle his feet as he walked. He lived with a Quaker family and attended the Buckingham Friends School.[159]

The Trusty family did not have manumission papers. They had been bound to the Spencer family—for their safety, to protect them against kidnappers or because they had a lifetime agreement with Colonel Spencer. In some way, that agreement changed when William and Ury Spencer inherited them. This question remains unanswered. This is how Levi learned to read and write. He was taught in the same classrooms as white children and freed or escaping black children. His father felt that he was still too close to slavery, since neighboring New Jersey remained a slaveholding state until 1846. Joseph Trusty and his family moved farther north after staying one year in Centerville. For this trip, the family traveled south on the Delaware Canal on the Pennsylvania side, passing through Quaker communities to Trenton, New Jersey. A map of the state of New Jersey shows a system of interwoven roads, links running from west to east to New York. The Hicksite Quaker communities provided the connections for the safe passage through Princeton to New Brunswick. From here, the connection may have been through Newark or Perth Amboy, where safe passage was made by boat to New York City.[160]

James McCune Smith wrote that when the family arrived in New York City, they underwent their "own metamorphosis, shedding the old reminders of subordination as a prelude to a new life. The father, in a simple ceremony conducted at home, proclaimed his family free, gave thanks to God, and renamed every member. 'Wife, they used to call you Henny (Henrietta) but now in the future your name is Elizabeth.' His daughter he renamed Eliza, his son Henry, and himself George."[161]

The family changed their last name to Garnet, modeled somewhat after Thomas Garret. Levi attended a new school with a new name (Henry Highland Garnet) on Mulberry Street in New York City. This school was one of many schools that was established by the Manumission Society in New York City. Henry was a student there from 1826 to 1828. In 1827, at the midpoint in Henry's school years, the New York legislature officially abolished slavery in New York State. Unfortunately, the ruling didn't mean that blacks, whether free men or runaway, were safe in New York. Runaways from Southern states where slavery was still legal could be grabbed off the street by a slave catcher, tried and, if convicted, returned to the South and slavery. Henry Garnet graduated from the African Free School and found a job as a ship's cabin boy. He had just returned from his second trip to Cuba when he learned that a slave catcher had come to his home and tried to grab his family as fugitives. His father had escaped by jumping out of a window. His mother had found refuge with friends who owned a grocery store across the street from the apartment. His sister, however, was arrested and put on trial as a fugitive from labor before Richard Riker, recorder of the city of New York. She managed to prove that she was a resident of New York and thus was released. The family's hard-earned possessions, however, had been completely destroyed.[162]

"The news brought Henry Garnet to the brink of madness." Henry purchased a clasp knife with the intention of finding the men who had come to New York to reclaim the family. He walked up and down Broadway swinging the knife back and forth to draw attention to himself. Fearing for his safety, a group of Quakers that had likely known him from the African Free School took him by wagon to the home of Thomas Willis. By the age of fourteen, Henry was as tall as some men. As a result, the trip to Jericho, Long Island, was made during the night so that he would not be noticed. The Willis home was nestled on a five-hundred-acre piece of property east of the

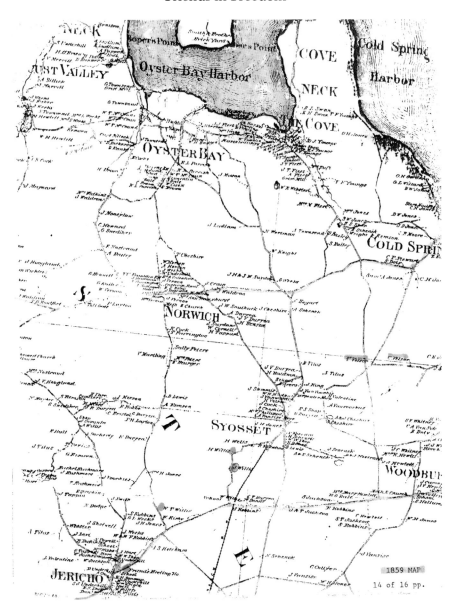

A map of Jericho, 1859. *Syosset Public Library.*

Jericho Meetinghouse and north of Jericho Turnpike. Henry stayed there for two weeks. He made a very positive impression on the Jericho Quaker community for his respectful manner and kind expressions. Henry was also very articulate and spoke with great passion about his disdain for the practice of enslaving one man to another. He spoke out against the political practices that allowed slave catchers to come across state lines to return human property to an owner. Perhaps this is why Elias Hicks came to visit Henry while he was staying at the Willis farm. The discussion influenced Henry for the rest of his life. After meeting Elias Hicks, a request was sent to other Quakers to find a temporary home for Henry until things were safe in New York City. An agreement was made to meet Epenetus Smith at the Jericho Meetinghouse.

Henry Garnet was then taken to Smithtown to the home and tavern of Epenetus Smith, one of the few Hicksite Quakers in the Smith family clan.[163] Despite the law freeing slaves in New York, proslavery sentiments ran high in Smithtown, and many people were still enslaved there. Henry Highland Garnet was very tall and would have found it difficult to just blend in with the other members of the community. A plan was made and an agreement signed that Henry would be indentured to Epenetus Smith for a period of time. Although Henry knew that he was free to go whenever he wanted to, he lived at the Smith home for two years. He worked at a sawmill located nearby. There were other enslaved people working there, and he was strong

Jericho Meetinghouse. *Velsor Collection.*

*Above*: The Epenetus Smith House. *Velsor Collection.*

*Right*: Henry Highland Garnet. *General Research & Reference Division, Schomburg Center for Black History and Culture, New York Public Library, Astor, Lenox and Tilden Foundations.*

and was a very good worker until he injured his leg with a saw at the mill. He suffered for a long time as his leg needed to heal properly. At this point, Henry threw his excess energy into his education and was tutored by Captain Epenetus Smith's son, Samuel. Eventually, he was reunited with his family, attended college and became a Presbyterian minister. An active abolitionist throughout his life, Henry Highland Garnet also served as a conductor on the Underground Railroad, operating his station out of the Liberty Street Presbyterian Church in Troy, New York.[164]

# The Underground Railroad Connection from North Carolina to Long Island

The connections made by Hicksite Quakers through their work in the Underground Railroad helped to establish a strong network for freedom seekers. One story that caught my attention early in my research was from a letter found by Queens historian James Driscoll. In 1834, Miles White, a member of the North Carolina Quakers Meeting, wrote to the Meeting for Sufferings that he had made arrangements for a group of "people of color under 'our' care" in New York and Brooklyn: "I ascertain that some friends at Jarico [Jericho], Long Island, were willing to receive and provide for a few families."[165]

The members of the Society of Friends in North Carolina fought hard against Southern political barriers to manumit their slaves. As slaves were freed, they were quickly picked up by slavers and resold. After 1791, when a slaveholder manumitted a slave, they had to post a bond for each. The price could vary from $100 to $1,000 depending on the court decision. The bond was used to harass Quakers. By 1808, matters had reached an impasse. In a slaveholding state, a black person needed to be protected from police and the courts. With the help of Judge William Gaston, a Catholic who abhorred slavery, a novel solution was made when the courts ruled that the North Carolina Yearly Meeting of Friends could become the owners of freed slaves. "The courts ruled that the slaves were property and not legal persons under the law and churches were allowed to hold property."[166]

The provision meant that these people would not be treated as slaves and would be paid for their work, and families could live together. The project was successful. More Quakers and non-Quakers deeded their slaves to the Yearly

Meeting. By 1814, the population had increased so much that the group became known as the Quaker Free Negroes. To deal with the enormous need for care, the Yearly Meeting created a Meeting for Sufferings. The number of people grew, and by 1824, a plan had been made to send a group to Haiti. When the members of the group found that Haiti was not a good place to live, they wrote back to the Meeting for Sufferings warning others not travel to Haiti. The second attempt was made to deliver a group to Liberia; this effort was known as the American Colonization Society. The expense of keeping the families was more than the North Carolina Yearly Meeting could afford, and sending them away in large groups seemed to be the solution.

A national appeal was sent out to Quaker Meetings across the free Northern states to send money and offer homes to these people. The first group left for an island of Liberia in 1827. The trip was made from Norfolk, Virginia. The families traveled from North Carolina by wagon, and then they boarded three ships. In 1828, the expense was too demanding, and with blacks in the North obtaining their freedom, a change in attitude came to those in North Carolina. Relocation to Liberia became less popular as reports came back that the effort was not successful. Another plan had to be made. In 1833, the Tappan brothers decided not to fund the project and threw their support to the abolition movement. The decision was made by the Meeting for Sufferings to move the family groups by wagon to the free states of Ohio, Indiana and Illinois. Many men volunteered to move groups to new destinations.[167]

A false-bottom wagon, Mendelson Museum. *Velsor Collection.*

Powell House, Bethpage Historical Village. *Nassau County Historical Collection.*

Mill Hill House. *Nassau County Historical Collection.*

In the spring of 2005, I received a grant to travel to Greensboro, North Carolina, to research the extent to which these people traveled. I knew that an appeal for funding had been sent to the New York Yearly Meeting in July 1849.[168] The Quaker collection is housed in the library at Guilford College in Greensboro. The Meeting for Sufferings minutes contained a short entry dated 1835. Reporting that a request had been sent from David White to Thomas Willis asking for placement of twenty-seven people, Thomas Willis of Jericho agreed to accept the group. Hiram Hilty wrote about the trip, "That time he managed to leave one refugee in the city of Brotherly Love, but New York Friends gave a friendly welcome to the twenty seven others he brought with him."[169]

The group was brought to Jericho under the care of Valentine Hicks. It was almost a disaster. There were too many of them and too many close encounters with slave catchers. By 1835, it had become very dangerous for such a large group of fugitives to travel to Long Island. It was more dangerous for them to travel than it was for the people who were helping them. If a fugitive were caught, they could be killed on sight. "They would have to pay the price." They were hanged or shackled to a tree and left to die. Sometimes they would just chop off the head of the fugitive and take it back south to show others not to run away. Families were drowned. The slave catcher would come back and just say that they found them but that they all died. It was too expensive and too dangerous to try and take them back south. Valentine noted that their courage was much greater than his. This is the reason Valentine decided to separate the family members into different homes until some connections were made. A group of twenty-eight blacks would have been difficult to hide just among the families in the Jericho Meeting.[170]

An appeal was extended to the Bethpage Meeting, and some family members went to the Thomas Powell farm, now located in Old Bethpage Village. The land today encompasses Bethpage, Plainview and Farmingdale. Although this large group seemed to be free blacks, they were actually fugitives. This meant that the families had to be relocated in Canada. An extensive effort was made by all of the members of the New York Meeting to relocate the group safely. The first step of the journey was made by a convoy of sorts from Oyster Bay Harbor. Several boats were needed. Valentine Hicks organized the escape. In 1836, the group was moved across Long Island Sound with the assistance of George C. Townsend.[171]

# Epilogue

Miracles bear witness to truth. They are convincing because they arise from conviction. Without conviction, they deteriorate.[172] The story of how the Quakers of Long Island helped enslaved people to freedom should no longer be subject to speculation. Whether the Quakers originated the effort to encourage enslaved Africans to free themselves or whether it is an event that happened because enslaved Africans knew that they would be safe at the home of a Quaker remains hidden from the records. The Quakers believed that God can speak directly to any person. Consequently, if a slave should appear at the doorstep of a Quaker's home or was seen walking alone without papers, the Quakers may have interpreted the presence of the enslaved person as a message from God to help a fellow friend to safety. This is how the events initially took place—not by political action but rather out of a mutual understanding of oppression and the underlying belief that all people are created equally. This is a story that began here on Long Island through the religious convictions of Elias Hicks. These convictions acted on through his ministry. His followers created the pathways to freedom that crossed the boundaries of slaveholding states, coming north to the small villages on Long Island. Transportation was then given to other Hicksite communities as groups of freedom seekers found refuge in other Quaker homes until they found freedom.

"A miracle is a service. It is the maximal service you can render to another. It is a way of loving your neighbor as yourself. You recognize your own and your neighbor's worth simultaneously."[173]

# NOTES

## INTRODUCTION

1. Letter to Wilmer, August 4, 1939.
2. Shultz, *Colonial Hempstead*, 145.

## THE SOCIETY OF FRIENDS ON LONG ISLAND

3. Cornell, *Adam and Anne Mott*, ii.
4. Barbour et al., *Quaker Crosscurrents*, 6–8.
5. *Rise and Growth*, 6.
6. Ibid.; Barbour et al., *Quaker Crosscurrents*, 6.
7. Barbour et al., *Quaker Crosscurrents*, 6.
8. Ibid.
9. Ibid.
10. *Flushing Remonstrance*, December 27, 1657.
11. *Rise and Growth*, 94.
12. Harrington, *George Fox*, 7, 9.
13. Ibid., 10–11.
14. Barbour et al., *Quaker Crosscurrents*, 65.
15. Ibid.
16. "Mennonites," http://www.answers.com/topic/mennonites, Gale Encyclopedia of U.S. History section.
17. Ibid.
18. Hicks family papers.

19. Barbour et al., *Quaker Crosscurrents*, 65.
20. See Lowry, *Story of the Flushing Meeting House*.
21. Barbour et al., *Quaker Crosscurrents*, 66.
22. Ibid., 28–29.
23. Wilson, "Quaker Hill Sociological Study," 41.
24. Ibid., 26.
25. Ibid.
26. Forbush, *Elias Hicks*, 78.
27. Barbour et al., *Quaker Crosscurrents*, 66.
28. See Hicks, "Freeing of Slaves on Long Island"; Hicks family papers.
29. Martin, "Hicks Family on Quakers," 88; Hicks family papers.
30. See Hicks, "Freeing of Slaves on Long Island"; Hicks family papers.
31. Barbour et al., *Quaker Crosscurrents*, 63.
32. Lowry, *Story of the Flushing Meeting House*, 14.
33. Martin, "Hicks Family on Quakers," 88; Hicks family papers.
34. Martin, "Hicks Family on Quakers," 88, 100; Hicks family papers.

# The First Free Black Communities on Long Island

35. Hodges, *Root & Branch*, 7–8.
36. Ibid.
37. Hartell, "Slavery on Long Island," 55; Onderdonk, *Long Island in the Olden Times*.
38. Hartell, "Slavery on Long Island," 55.
39. Ibid.
40. Wilson, *New York City's African Slaveowners*, 43.
41. See Woodson, *Mind of the Negro*.
42. Hartell, "Slavery on Long Island," 61; Onderdonk, *Long Island in the Olden Times*.
43. Hartell, "Slavery on Long Island," 62; Onderdonk, *Long Island in the Olden Times*.
44. Martin, "Hicks Family on Quakers," 85; Hartell, "Slavery on Long Island," 62.
45. Hartell, "Slavery on Long Island," 62.
46. Onderdonk, *Long Island in the Olden Times*.
47. Ibid.
48. Hartell, "Slavery on Long Island," 62; Onderdonk, *Long Island in the Olden Times*.
49. Hartell, "Slavery on Long Island," 62.
50. Onderdonk, *Long Island in the Olden Times*.

51. Ibid.
52. Ibid.
53. Marcus, *Discovering the African American Experience*, 93–125.
54. Onderdonk, *Long Island in the Olden Times.*
55. Ibid.
56. Ibid.
57. Prude, "To Look Upon the 'Lower Sort,'" 124–57.
58. Onderdonk, *Long Island in the Olden Times.*
59. Prude, "To Look Upon the 'Lower Sort,'" 124–57.
60. Ibid. The table is in seven groups, with the ads by years 1716–50, 1752–60, 1761–75 and 1776–83.
61. Hartell, "Slavery on Long Island," 62.
62. Ibid.

# Elias Hicks

63.. Forbush, *Elias Hicks*, 145–46.
64. Ibid., 3–4.
65. Ibid., 17–18.
66. Ibid., 24.
67. Ibid., 28.
68. Ibid., 31.
69. Ibid.
70. Ibid.
71. Hicks, "Freeing of Slaves on Long Island."
72. Martin, "Hicks Family on Quakers"; Hicks, "Freeing of Slaves on Long Island."
73. Barbour et al., *Quaker Crosscurrents*, 74; Gaines, *Charity Society*, 2.
74. Barbour, *Slavery and Theology*, 4.
75. "Prize goods" were goods made by slaves, such as sugar, coffee, cotton and rice. Forbush, *Elias Hicks*, 144.
76. Drake, *Quakers and Slavery*, 116; Forbush, *Elias Hicks*, 145.
77. Hicks, *Observations on the Slavery*, 4, 5, 7–9, 20–22; Forbush, *Elias Hicks*, 147–48.
78. Forbush, *Elias Hicks*, 145–48.
79. James Mott was the son of John Mott, member of the Westbury Meeting. The Old Mott Homestead was a station on the Underground Railroad in Sands Point, Long Island, on Hempstead Harbor, running across to Premium Point in Westchester County, New York.
80. Drake, *Quakers and Slavery*, 117.
81. In 1827–28, the views and popularity of Elias Hicks resulted in a division within five Yearly Meetings: Philadelphia, New York, Ohio, Indiana and

Baltimore. Rural Friends, who had increasingly chafed under the control of urban leaders, sided with Hicks and naturally took a stand against strong discipline in doctrinal questions.

82. Barbour et al., *Quaker Crosscurrents*, 73; Murphy, *Jericho*, 42–45.
83. Forbush, *Elias Hicks*, 4.
84. Ibid., 145–47.
85. Barbour et al., *Quaker Crosscurrents*, 74; Forbush, *Elias Hicks*, 4.

## QUAKER FAMILIES AND THEIR CONNECTIONS

86. Cornell, *Adam and Anne Mott*, 12.
87. Ibid., 12–13.
88. Ibid., 2.
89. Ibid., 25–26
90. Ibid., 26.

## JERUSALEM

91. Wantagh was originally called "Jerusalem" and was located on the Jerusalem River. Today, it is called Bellmore Creek.
92. Robbins, *History of the Jackson Family*, 177.
93. Ibid.
94. See McKennan and Peppe, *Wantagh Past and Present*.
95. Powell, "Family Records," 4. Logic alone supports the transport to the Jackson family on the southern shore of Long Island. The Jacksons were related through marriage and were all members of the Society of Friends.
96. Thomas was the son of Pannenas and Charity Coles Jackson. His grandfather was John Jackson, third-generation cousin to Obadiah Jackson of Jericho. Robbins, *History of the Jackson Family*, property deed.
97. McKennan, *Wantagh Past and Present*, 10–12.

## JERICHO

98. Letter from Mary Willis to Amy Post, 1838, Post family letters.
99. Hicks family papers.
100. Cornell, *Anne and Adam Mott*, 373.
101. Cox, *Quakerism*, 180–82.
102. Winsche, "Historic Buildings Evaluation." The building is now the Maine Maid Inn. In an examination of the existing floors in the dining room, I discovered three boards that were placed against the north wall. I unscrewed the boards and found a hollow space that is believed to have

been a hiding place for the architectural drawings of the secret staircase. It seems some modifications were made to the stairs by a recent restaurant owner. The door still remains in the hallway with the secret staircase.

103. Martin, "Hicks Family on Quakers," 186–89.

104. Hicks, "Freeing of Slaves on Long Island."

105. Hicks family papers; see McAllister, "Family Affairs."

106. Tyson, "Some Items"; Hicks family papers. This story has been told and retold to family members about the work of Valentine and Abigail Hicks.

107. Forbush, *Elias Hicks*, 38.

108. Close examination of the foundation of the original fireplace revealed a number of inconsistencies. There are beams running under the structure, there is a hole in the original floorboards so that you can see the room above the stone structure, there is a noisy steel plate in the floor of the dining room that moves when it is stepped on. The east wall in the basement to the left of the stone structure has a hole in it that reveals blue stones that may have been used to fill in the root cellar. Hicks family papers.

109. Letter from Mary Robbins Post, 18?2, to Isaac Post, Post family letters; Hicks family papers.

110. Robbins, *History of the Jackson Family*, 177; e-mail from Betsey Murphy, historian, Jericho Public Library.

111. McAllister, "Family Affairs," 31–32.

112. Ibid., 34.

113. Letter from Mary Jackson to Hanna Post, 1823, Post family letters; Letter to Mary Willis to Amy Post, 1838, Post family letters.

114. From a walking tour of the Malcolm Home in the spring of 2012.

115. Hicks family papers; McAllister, "Family Affairs," 31–32.

116. The Mill Pond House is the original home of John Townsend and is on the north side of the Mill Pond in Oyster Bay. The Mill Hill House is on the east side of the Mill Pond. This house was originally a barn and was made into a house during the 1840s.

117. Christopher Densmore e-mail, August 13, 2012, reported that G.W. Townsend was disowned in 1828 for having a child out of wedlock. Further research connected me to a story that the members of the Jericho Meeting did not feel that his request for payment was consistent with being a Friend. Hicks family papers.

118. Valentine Hicks, Hicks family papers.

## OLD WESTBURY

119. Day, "Friends in the Spirit," 7.

120. Cornell, *Anne and Adam Mott*, 300. Phebe was the daughter of Benjamin Seaman of Jerusalem.

121. Ibid., 373.
122. Ibid.
123. Manumission Society minutes, Roll 1.
124. Ibid.
125. Martin, "Hicks Family on Quakers," 62.
126. It is now the AME Zion Church in New Cassel on Brush Hollow Road. Emory, "History of Long Island."
127. Hicks family papers.
128. Ibid.
129. Ibid.
130. Martin, "Hicks Family on Quakers," 170.
131. Hicks family papers.
132. Abbott, *Post, Albertson, & Hicks*, xxiv–xxv.
133. Ibid., 168.
134. The suitcase is part of the permanent collection in the Westbury Historical Society. The newspapers are in a collection in the Society for the Preservation of Long Island Antiquities.
135. Powell, *Personal Reminiscences*, 155–59.
136. Emory, "History of Long Island"; letter from Mary Robbins Post to Isaac Post, 1848, Post family letters.
137. Hicks family papers.
138. Valentine and Abigail Hicks had five children who were simultaneously siblings and cousins. They named one of their sons Elias Hicks. Born in 1815, this Elias Hicks also married a Hicks: Sarah Hicks, the daughter of Robert Hicks and Mary Underhill Mott Hicks. Isaac and Sarah Hicks had six children: John D., Robert, Benjamin, Isaac, Elizabeth and Mary. Isaac Hicks's sons Robert Hicks and Isaac Hicks became business partners. Like their father and Uncle Valentine, both were active New York abolitionists.
139. Cornell, *Anne and Adam Mott*, 375. Against his father's wishes, Robert Hicks built his home at 46 (afterward 54) Market Street, New York City, and went into the ship chandelier business with Captain Laban Gardiner. Soon after forming the partnership, Gardiner retired, and Robert Hicks went into partnership with his brother Benjamin. When Benjamin Hicks died in 1835, Robert brought his two remaining brothers—John and Isaac—into the business, which he inexplicably renamed Robert Hicks and Sons. In 1839 or 1840, the building burned down. Hicks moved operations to Burling Slip, located on the East River, at the foot of Fulton Street. Cornell, *Anne and Adam Mott*, 375–76.
140. Powell, *Personal Reminiscences*, 160.
141. Ibid.

## THE STORY OF LEVI TRUSTY

142. "New Market Square" is a reference to the architectural layout of the community.

143. First Census for the United States, Maryland, 84, lists William Spencer family from New Market as having two white males, one under ten years of age and one between the ages of twenty-six and forty-five. The census shows two white females, one under ten years of age and one between the ages of twenty-six and forty-five. Two members are involved in agriculture and one in manufacturing. The census identifies two slaves over forty-five and seven other persons (except Indian) not taxed.

144. Smith and Wilson, "Memorial Discourse," 17–35.

145. Ibid.

146. Williams and McKinsey, *History of Frederick County*, 326.

147. Ibid.

148. Jacobsen, *Quaker Records*, publication no. 14.

149. Barbour et al., *Quaker Crosscurrents*, 66–67, 136.

150. *Frederick Town Herald*, 1820–24.

151. First Census for the United States, Maryland, 87.

152. Frederick County, Maryland, land records, WR36.

153. Smith and Wilson, "Memorial Discourse," 17–35.

154. The Deer Creek Meeting belonged to the Nottingham Quarterly Meeting and, thus, the Philadelphia Yearly Meeting.

155. Jacobsen, *Quaker Records*, publication no. 14. The Bush Creek Meetinghouse was part of the Nottingham Meeting. The Nottingham Yearly Meetings were held in Philadelphia. During the separation, the Baltimore Meeting, which included Gun Powder Falls and Little Falls, and the Nottingham Meeting were all Hicksite Meetings.

156. Smith and Wilson, "Memorial Discourse," 20. This is the barn that Harriet Tubman used as she ran to freedom and the same connection that she used when helping others to make their way north.

157. Blockson, *Underground Railroad*, 35.

158. Mount Gilead AME Church, Mount Gilead, Buckingham, Pennsylvania.

159. *Buckingham School* pamphlet, 6. The Buckingham School was authorized in 1794 to establish a fund to educate their children, as well as to educate the children of those who were "bound apprentices of the members of the meeting." Within two years, the Monthly Meeting was on record as having a school for educating free blacks and Indians.

160. Switala, *Underground Railroad*, 39.

161. Smith and Wilson, "Memorial Discourse," 20.

162. Ibid., 25–26.

163. Ibid., 26.

164. Ibid. The Epenetus Smith Tavern is owned by the Smithtown Historical District and stands on the north side of Route 25A just west of Route 111 in Smithtown. Driscoll et al., *Friends of Freedom.*

## THE UNDERGROUND RAILROAD CONNECTION FROM NORTH CAROLINA TO LONG ISLAND

165. Driscoll et al., *Friends of Freedom*, 56.
166. Hilty, *By Land and by Sea*, 31–32.
167. Ibid., 44–69.
168. Letter from William Harned to members of the New York Meeting, July 28, 1849, Queens Historical Society Collection.
169. Hilty, *By Land and by Sea*, 71; Meeting for Sufferings minutes, 1835, Guilford College Library.
170. Hicks family papers; personal meeting with Leon Rushmore.
171. *Rural Heritage for Today.*

## EPILOGUE

172. Foundation for Inner Peace, *Course in Miracles*, 2.
173. Ibid.

# BIBLIOGRAPHY

## BOOKS

Abbott, Margery Post, ed. *Post, Albertson, & Hicks Family Papers.* Centralia, WA, 2009.

Barbour, Hugh. *Slavery and Theology: Writings of Seven Quaker Reformers, 1800 to 1870.* Dublin, IN, 1985.

Barbour, Hugh, Christopher Densmore, Elizabeth H. Moger, Nancy C. Sorel, Alson D. Van Wagner and Arthur J. Worrall. *Quaker Crosscurrents: Three Hundred Years of Friends in the New York Yearly Meeting.* Syracuse, NY, 1999.

Blockson, Charles L. *The Underground Railroad in Pennsylvania.* Jacksonville, NC: Flame International, 1981.

Cornell, Thomas Clapp. *Adam and Anne Mott: Their Ancestors and Their Descendants.* Poughkeepsie, NY, 1809.

Cox, John J. *Quakerism in the City of New York, 1657–1930.* New York: privately printed, 1930.

Day, Lynda. *Making a Way to Freedom.* Interlaken, NY, 1997.

Drake, Thomas. *Quakers and Slavery in America.* New Haven, CT, 1950.

Driscoll, James, Derek M. Grey, Richard Hourahan and Kathleen G. Velsor. *Angels of Deliverance: The Underground Railroad in Queens and Long Island.* Flushing, NY, 1999.

———. *Friends of Freedom: The Underground Railroad in Queens and Long Island.* Flushing, NY, 2006.

Forbush, Bliss. *Elias Hicks, Quaker Liberal.* New York, 1956.

Forbush, William. *Wantagh, Jerusalem and Ridgewood, 1664–1897*. Jamaica, NY, 1892.

Foundation for Inner Peace. *A Course in Miracles*. Glen Ellen, CA, 1976.

Harrington, R.W. *George Fox at Flushing and Oyster Bay*. Long Island, NY, 1652.

Hicks, Elias. *Observations on the Slavery of Africans and Their Descendants*. New York, 1811.

———. *A Series of Extemporaneous Discourses*. Philadelphia, PA, 1825.

Hilty, Hiram H. *By Land and by Sea: Quakers Confront Slavery and Its Aftermath in North Carolina*. Greensboro, NC, 1993.

———. *New Garden Friends Meeting: The Christian People Called Quakers*. Greensboro, NC, 2001.

Hodges, Graham. *Root & Branch: African Americans in New York and East Jersey, 1613–1863*. Chapel Hill: University of North Carolina Press, 1999.

Irvin, Francis. *Oyster Bay Sketch Book*. Oyster Bay, NY, 1987.

Jacobsen, Phebe R. *Quaker Records in Maryland*. Hall of Records Commission State of Maryland Yearly Meeting, Baltimore, MD, 1866.

Lowry, Ann. *The Story of the Flushing Meeting House*. Flushing, NY, 1994.

Marcus, Grania. *Discovering the African American Experience in Suffolk County, 1620–1860*. Cold Spring Harbor, NY, 1995.

Mott, Abigail. *Biographical Sketches and Interesting Anecdotes of Persons of Color*. New York, 1837.

Murphy, Betsey. *Jericho: The History of a Long Island Hamlet*. Jericho, NY, 2009.

Powell, Aaron. *Personal Reminiscences of the Anti-Slavery Movement and Other Reforms and Reformers*. New York, 1899.

*Rise and Growth of the Society of Friends on Long Island and New York, 1657 to 1826*. Reprinted in Henry Onderdonk Jr.'s *Annual of Hempstead, 1643–1832*. New York, 1878.

Robbins, Oscar Burton. *History of the Jackson Family of Hempstead, Long Island, N.Y., Ohio and Indiana: Descendants of Robert and Agnes Washburn Jackson*. Ohio, 1951.

Schor, Joel. *Henry Highland Garnet: A Voice of Black Radicalism in the Nineteenth Century*. Westport, CT, 1977.

Schultz, Bernice. *Colonial Hempstead*. Lynbrook, NY, 1937.

Seng, Joseph F. *Back When: The Story of Historic New Market, Maryland*. Westminster, MD, 2005.

Smith, James McCune, MD, and Joseph M. Wilson. "Memorial Discourse, by Reverend Henry Highland Garnet." Philadelphia, PA, 1865.

Switala, William. *The Underground Railroad in New York and New Jersey*. Mechanicsburg, PA, 2006.

Williams, T.J.C., and Folger McKinsey. *History of Frederick County.* Chicago, 1967.

Wilson, Sherill. *New York City's African Slaveowners: A Social Material Culture History.* New York, 1994.

Woodson, Carter Godwin. *Mind of the Negro as Reflected in Letters Written During the Crisis of 1800–1860.* New York, 2010.

# NEWSPAPERS

*Daily News*
*Frederick Town Herald*
*Long Island Farmer*
*New York Gazette*
*New York Mercury*

# PAMPHLETS AND BROCHURES

*Buckingham School, 1794–1994.* Lahaska, PA: Buckingham School, 1994.

*Flushing Remonstrance.* Flushing, NY: Coalition for a Planned Flushing, New York, 1993.

Friends of Long Island Heritage. *A Rural Heritage for Today: A Guide to Old Bethpage Village Restoration.* New York: Nassau County Department of Parks and Recreation, 1990.

Gaines, Edith. *The Charity Society, 1794–1994.* Jericho, NY: self-published, 1994.

McKennan, Gordon, and Allen Peppe. *Wantagh Past and Present.* Wantagh, NY, 1966.

# ARTICLES

Day, Lynda R. "Friends in the Spirit: African Americans and the Challenge to Quaker Liberalism, 1776–1915." *Long Island Historical Journal* 10, no. 1 (1994).

Hartell, Anne. "Slavery on Long Island." *Long Island Historical Journal* 6, no. 2 (1943): 55.

Jackson, Marion. "Old Jericho and Its Quakers." *Nassau County Journal* (1980). Reprint, Jericho Public Library.

Prude, Johnathan. "To Look Upon the 'Lower Sort': Runaway Ads and the Appearance of Unfree Laborers in America, 1750–1800." *Journal of American History* (June 1991): 124–57.

# DISSERTATIONS

Martin, Sister Mary, RSM. "The Hicks Family on Quakers, Farmer and Entrepreneurs." PhD diss., St. John's University, 1976.

Wilson, Warren, AM. "Quaker Hill Sociological Study." PhD diss., Columbia University, 1907.

# LETTERS AND SPEECHES

Hicks, Henry. "Freeing of Slaves on Long Island by Members of the Religious Society of Friends or Quakers and Self Help Organization Among Colored People." Speech given by Hicks at the celebration of the seventy-seventh anniversary of the Freeing of the Slaves Organization, sponsored by the Westbury AME Zion Church and held at Fireman's Hall on January 9, 1941. Typescript located in the Historical Society of the Westbury Archives.

Pierce, Johnathan Carpenter. Letter written on August 4, 1939. Swarthmore College Library, Havilland Record Room, Swarthmore, Pennsylvania.

Post family letters. University of Rochester, Rheese Library, Rochester, New York.

# MINUTES OF MEETINGS

Manumission Society minutes, Roll 1, New York Historical Society.

# HISTORICAL RECORDS

First Census for the United States, Maryland. Frederick Historical Society, Maryland.

Frederick County, Maryland, land records, WR36. Fredrick Courthouse, Maryland.

New York Manumission Society records. New York Historical Society.

# MISCELLANEOUS

Emory, Ester. "History of Long Island: Old Westbury." Westbury Historical Collection, Westbury, New York.

Hicks family papers. Westbury Historical Collection, Westbury, New York. Private collections.

Jackson family papers. Wantagh Public Library, Wantagh, New York.

Jericho Public Library, 1939.

McAllister, Phebe Ketchum. "Family Affairs, or Go to Jericho, Concerning the Family Events and Traditions, Childhood Memoirs and Later Experiences, Family Life and Heritage as Recorded by Phebe Ketchum McAllister."

Onderdonk, Henry. *Long Island in the Olden Times.* A collection of newspaper clippings, New York Public Library.

Powell, Fred J. "Family Records and Personal Reminiscences." Queens Historical Society, Queens, New York. Private collection of Nina Powell.

Renison, Jean. "Conversations and Hand Written Notes on the History of Westbury." Westbury Historical Collection, Westbury, New York.

Tyson, William Hawxhurst. "Some Items that Might Be of Interest to Corrine." Westbury Historical Society, Westbury, New York.

Winsche, Richard A. "Historic Buildings Evaluation." Jericho Public Library. Jericho, New York.

# INDEX

# ABOUT THE AUTHOR

D r. Kathleen Gaffney Velsor is currently an associate professor in the School of Education at the State University of New York– Old Westbury. She earned an undergraduate degree in fine arts and education from Lindenwood University in St. Charles, Missouri, and received her master's degree in educational administration from Lehigh University in Pennsylvania and her doctorate in educational research from the University of Cincinnati in Ohio. She has received numerous grants to research the Quaker involvement in the Underground Railroad on Long Island, most recent among them an education grant from the Long Island Community Foundation to establish the Underground Teaching Partnership to build community through interdisciplinary social studies workshops for schoolteachers.

In her research supporting the Underground Railroad, she has published a historical novel for young adult readers, *Brother & Me* (Rosalie Ink, 2005). She has also published three books—*Friends of Freedom: The Underground Railroad in Queens, Long Island and Beyond* (2006); *The Road to Freedom* (2001), a supplemental text for seventh graders; and *Angel of Deliverance: The Underground*

*Railroad in Queens, Long Island* (1999)—all published by the Queens Historical Society. Two articles of hers appeared in the *Afro-American Historical and Genealogical Society Journal*: "The Long Island Freedom Trail" (vol. 23, Spring 2004) and "Sketch of the Life and Labors of Rev. Henry Highland Garnet: A Second Look" (vol. 26, Spring 2009).

Dr. Velsor teaches undergraduate courses in the Department of Elementary Education and Literacy. She teaches courses for preservice teachers in children's literature, child development and reading. Kathleen lives with her family in Bayville, New York.